T0146986

THE
DIGNITY MINDSET:
A LEADER'S GUIDE TO BUILDING GENDER EQUITY AT WORK

THE
DIGNITY
MINDSET:
A LEADER'S GUIDE TO BUILDING GENDER EQUITY AT WORK

SUSAN HODGKINSON

THE DIGNITY MINDSET: A LEADER'S GUIDE TO BUILDING GENDER EQUITY AT WORK

iUniverse books may be ordered through booksellers or by contacting:

iUniverse
1663 Liberty Drive
Bloomington, IN 47403
www.iuniverse.com
1-800-Authors (1-800-288-4677)

ISBN: 978-1-5320-7516-2 (sc)
ISBN: 978-1-5320-7517-9 (hc)
ISBN: 978-1-5320-7515-5 (e)

Library of Congress Control Number: 2019908295

Print information available on the last page.

iUniverse rev. date: 07/11/2019

DEDICATION

To Alesia Latson, my beloved colleague and friend. The power of her brilliant work has lifted the lives of so many. She is proof angels live among us.

ACKNOWLEDGMENTS

To the women of color who have shaped my worldview and whose spirit and perseverance in the face of daily adversity inspired me to write this book. Your dignity, your elegance, and your resilience are an unparalleled example to us all.

To Alice Lesch Kelly, world-class writer, whose writing and editorial skills added tremendous value to this book.

With special thanks to Gisela Marx and her tireless capacity for listening, encouraging, and reframing over the three years of effort that resulted in this book.

For

Lovely Day
Piper
Precious Bird

CONTENTS

PART I
Understanding Gender Bias

INTRODUCTION

From Hegemony to Dignity

"Gender parity is not just good for women—it's good for societies."

— Angélica Fuentes, Mexican businesswoman,
philanthropist, and gender equality activist

About four years ago I was invited to give a keynote speech at a prestigious all-women's business conference. It was a huge honor, and I was thrilled to have the opportunity to address several hundred amazing businesswomen from all over the United States. When the conference sponsor asked me to talk about the future of women in the workplace, I agreed immediately— it's a topic that fires me up as a woman and a business coach. But then the sponsor added a request that made me hesitate: To deliver an optimistic speech.

Well. The American workplace has a long way to go in terms of gender equity, and I wasn't about to ignore that. But we've made so much progress, right? Certainly, there were plenty of great examples that I could include in my keynote of situations in which women were flourishing in gender-balanced organizations. Sure, I told the sponsor. I'd give the speech an optimistic spin.

Then I started my research. What I found left me feeling anything but optimistic. Despite the efforts of so many well-meaning people, the percentage of women on corporate boards in the U.S. wasn't really improving. The gender pay gap was holding steady. The number of female

1

CEOs was barely budging. And I knew from the stories I heard regularly from my business coaching clients that even when women did land positions as top executives or on corporate boards, they often felt like outsiders in mostly male boardrooms.

How could I possibly be optimistic about the future of women in the workplace when so many signs pointed to a depressing lack of progress?

I started looking outside the U.S., and when I considered the inroads women have made on the international stage, my optimism began to surge. German Chancellor Angela Merkel has been called the most powerful woman in the world. Christine Lagarde influences monetary policy throughout the world as chair of the International Monetary Fund. The HeForShe solidarity campaign initiated by the United Nations is making meaningful progress advancing gender equality and fighting negative stereotypes and behaviors in many countries. On a smaller scale, women are making huge advances at all levels of their workplaces in countries such as Iceland, Denmark, Australia, and Canada. I even found reasons to feel optimistic about gender inclusion in certain developing countries, where women are making some astonishing strides despite huge barriers.

As I considered these examples I wondered, why aren't we accomplishing more in the U.S.? What's standing in our way? It's not that organizations in the U.S. aren't trying to increase gender equity. Many offer training sessions and create mentorship programs and set aggressive inclusion goals. And yet, we're not really moving the needle. Why?

I couldn't answer that question when I delivered that keynote speech four years ago. But I can answer it now. After wrapping up my talk, I devoted myself to understanding this problem and uncovering its solutions. I started digging, digging, digging, researching and reading, talking with experts, analyzing reports, and soaking up success stories.

This book is the culmination of that research. It is an in-depth look at why true gender balance in the workplace has eluded us in the U.S. and how we can make the fundamental changes necessary to have more inclusive workplaces, where women can feel free to use their talents to drive organizational success.

And in case you think that only women will benefit from this transformation, let me set your mind to rest. Rock-solid research shows that when women have the freedom to contribute equitably in a workplace, their success raises the entire organization. Profits go up. Customer satisfaction increases. And yes, even the men are happier. A rising tide of gender equity in the workplace lifts every part of the organization.

Four years after giving that speech, I feel more optimistic than ever before about how to make U.S. workplaces more gender inclusive. That's because I understand why this is such a problem for us, and I know the roadmap we can follow to make things better.

My purpose in writing this book is to share that roadmap with you so you can bring about transformative change in your workplace. Whether you're a man or a woman, a CEO or a budding leader, you can use the information in this book to guide your organization in an exciting new direction: toward a belief system that paves the way to gender balance.

A Ubiquitous Belief System

I am an executive coach and the founder of The Personal Brand Company, a leadership development firm that has helped thousands of professionals in diverse industries become more effective leaders. My team and I work with talented, values-driven clients—women and men—who want to achieve success for themselves and their organizations.

As an executive coach, I'm privy to many of the inner struggles that keep leaders up at night. Two of those struggles reinforced my desire to research and write this book over the past four years.

I'll start with something I often hear from men. An uncountable number of well-meaning male executives have told me that they'd love to hire more women for top positions, but they struggle to find and retain talented women. These executives are frustrated, because they recognize the value of having women on management teams, they support their organizations' diversity efforts, and they devote significant resources to creating gender-inclusive teams. But still, they struggle to attract and keep women in their management ranks.

Now, to the women: I can't tell you how often brilliant, talented, successful women who hold top-level positions in major U.S. organizations have confessed to me that they feel like frauds at work. Even though their resumes and any quantitative evaluation of their performances reveal a stratospheric level of accomplishment, these women spend many of their hours at work feeling sick with fear. They stay quiet in meetings when they know they should speak up, they doubt the positive feedback they receive, they question their success, and they live with a nagging sense that at any moment, they will be exposed as being a complete and utter fraud. If you're a woman, you probably recognize these feelings of low confidence and "imposter syndrome," which are as prevalent as the common cold.

These two examples are different sides of the same problem, and they're at the core of the challenge of gender inequity in the workplace. They reflect the fact that we live in a society that is built around the belief that men are dominant and women are subordinate.

This belief goes by a few different names, such as the male hegemonic power myth or the male power belief system. And it can reach beyond gender, to race and sexual orientation. But at its core, it's a belief system that legitimizes the subordination of women because of the assumption that they simply aren't as valuable as men in society or in the workplace. This belief system creates a gender bias that is wired into us all and is reinforced throughout our lives.

It's not just men who buy into the male power belief system. Women have internalized it, too—it's the fuel that powers low confidence and imposter syndrome. It occurs when women see themselves through the frame of the male gaze, when women take on the male perspective in which they are subordinate beings who exist to support and please men, rather than to express their own identities. Because of the ubiquity of the male power belief system, we live in a world—and work in organizations— curated by men and framed by the male viewpoint, just as we have for thousands of years.

The male power belief system is a massive, dense structure that is as impermeable as cement. It's the reason that male CEOs have trouble hiring and retaining brilliant women on their management teams, and it's the reason that brilliant women doubt themselves even when they're accomplishing amazing things and may feel reluctant to pursue high-level opportunities. Because of the male power belief system, organizations remain stubbornly inequitable to women.

Moving Toward a Dignity Mindset

If the male power belief system really is so impervious, how are some countries and organizations getting around it? How is success possible?

Here's how. Success comes when leaders acknowledge the tentacled grip that the male power belief system has on our organizations and our society. By recognizing and naming it what it is—a system that not only harms women and men, but that holds organizations back as well—we can inch forward toward embracing a new belief system.

And once we begin to replace old, destructive beliefs with new, supportive beliefs, we can change the behaviors that trap us in our current unbalanced system.

When beliefs change, behaviors change. When a culture—corporate or societal—lets go of the ingrained belief that women are inferior to men, transformation can start. In this book I share some glorious examples of places that have transformed their belief systems and, in turn, their behaviors, freeing women to shine in a way that illuminates everything around them. I show you what you can learn from those places so you can follow their examples in your organization.

When we move away from the male power belief system, we free all our employees—men as well as women—to do amazing things. We make space for truly gender-balanced organizations in which all of our employees can flourish and have their fundamental human needs met, and we can reach our business goals. The male power belief system is bad for women, for men, and for business.

It's time for us to break away from that destructive belief system and adopt a new viewpoint that's based on a foundation of shared human dignity rather than male power and female subordination.

The pivotal concept here is dignity. Donna Hicks, PhD, a conflict resolution specialist at Harvard and one of my heroes, talks about dignity as a guiding star that can lead us to gender balance in our workplaces. She believes, as I do, that we all have a deep, human desire to be treated as something of value, and that this shared desire for dignity transcends all of our differences. When we recognize our shared identity—when we look at the workplace with a Dignity Mindset built around the belief that everyone has the same worth and the same fundamental needs as everyone else—conflicts between us can begin to disappear. In organizations, recognizing our shared identity as men and women—as equals, not as superiors and subordinates—allows us to move beyond the outmoded male power belief system and create dignity-based workplaces in which gender diversity not only makes sense, but can feel invigorating. When every person in an organization sees every other person in the organization as having equal value and worth, that's when things are really going to change.

A Roadmap for You

This book is for everyone who wants to create gender-balanced organizations and dignity-based workplaces where all employees can reach their potential. It's for women who want to stop feeling like imposters and men who recognize the tremendous value of inclusivity. My goal is to reach ambitious, open-minded leaders at every level who want to see authentic change in their organizations.

Men, hear this: Even though I blame the male power belief system for the situation we're in, I'm no male basher. I know there are men who want to continue subordinating women. But this book isn't for them—it's for the countess male leaders who want to create gender-balanced workplaces but simply don't know how. If that's you, I'm thrilled that you've picked up this book. I know it's tough being a woman in today's workplace, but I also know that men haven't had it easy lately, either.

This book's aim is to enable you to build and sustain an inclusive organization. Although its focus is on gender balance; its ideas apply to other populations that have been harmed by the male power belief system (and that I care deeply about), including people of color, the LGBTQ and gender non-binary community, those with disabilities, and anyone else treated as an outsider in their own organizations. I deeply honor and respect these people, but I will not presume to speak for them. They are in my mind, but in this book, I'll stick to what I know best: women.

I know we have our work cut out for us. But I feel more optimistic than ever before that change is within our reach. With this book as your roadmap, you're in a position to transform your organization. You and other leaders like you can make significant progress toward bringing gender balance and a Dignity Mindset to workplaces across the U.S. and throughout the world.

CHAPTER 1

The Myth Behind the Beliefs

"The first problem for all of us, men and women,
is not to learn, but to unlearn."

— Gloria Steinem

Two CEOs sit on a plane, waiting for takeoff. It's early evening, and the men are looking forward to going home after a long day of meetings. When the flight attendant offers drinks, they're quick to accept.

"I needed that," says the CEO in seat 2A as he takes a long sip of his bourbon on the rocks.

"Tough day?" asks his fellow traveler in 2B, who's settling in with a vodka tonic. "My meetings went great. But I just got a call from my COO telling me she's quitting to take a position at another company." He shakes his head. "I can't believe it—she's only been with us a year."

"Ugh. I feel your pain. Did she say why she's leaving?"

"She says the organization that recruited her is a more welcoming place for women than our company, whatever the hell that means. Sheesh. I hired her—isn't that welcoming enough? Went out of my way to find a woman because my HR people say we need more women in top jobs," says 2A, motioning to the flight attendant for a refill. "Took forever for us to hire her, and now she ups and leaves. I don't understand it."

"Yeah, we have the same problem. Tough to hire women, tough to keep them," says 2B, tearing open a bag of pretzels. "The thing is, I'm sold on this gender diversity thing. I used to think it was just politically correct BS, but when I started paying attention to the research, I realized we'd be crazy not to bring on more women. No question about it; gender diversity is linked to better financial performance. It really is a competitive advantage."

"And it's nice to have them around, right?" 2A says with a wink.

2B shakes his head. "That's outdated thinking, my friend. Not good for you or your company. It's about outlooks, not looks. I'm convinced—and the research backs me up— that women can bring viewpoints and perspectives that just don't surface in an all-male team. Listen, the majority of our customers are women, so we need women at every level of our organization to help us understand what these customers want."

"I suppose," 2A says. "Then why is it so hard to hire these women—and why don't they stay on the job once we give them a chance? They want us to take them seriously as executives, treat them like men, but it's hard to do that when they leave for no reason at all."

2B sighs. "Honestly, we've had some of the same experiences you've had. And it really puzzles me, because we're trying to do everything right. We've told our recruiters to make gender diversity a top priority. We try our best to have a woman on every team. We even formed a woman's employee resource group. We check all those boxes, but we still can't retain them. I'm not sure what else we can do."

2A and 2B are stumped, but the woman sitting directly in front of them, a biotech executive, has some ideas about why the women on their management teams don't feel welcome. She's thinking of leaving her position because her male CEO is a classic power hoarder. He hires women for executive roles—he's read the same McKinsey & Company reports on profitability and gender balance as the guy in 2B—but he doesn't really believe women are a crucial part of the executive team. She sees evidence of this on a regular basis. Her CEO forgets to send her critical emails and leaves her out of social events that all the "boys" on the team attend. During meetings, he frequently interrupts her and doesn't listen to or acknowledge her ideas. And he's just about the worst mansplainer she's ever come across. During a meeting last week, he paused the discussion to explain to her what a triple threat is in basketball even though she played on a Big Eight hoops team in college. Yes, she could certainly tell the boys in row 2 a few things about why women leave companies where they don't feel welcome.

And the woman sitting next to them could share some stories about what happens when women executives have the freedom to contribute in an authentic way. She's smiling to herself as she sips a glass of prosecco and thinks about the meeting she attended today.

She sits on the board of a Fortune 500 consumer products company that truly believes in diversity and that has made a strong effort to recruit women to its board. Currently 43% of the company's directors are women, which is more than double the 2018 average in Fortune 500 companies overall.[1] Since the company increased the number of women on its board, return on equity and earnings per share have increased significantly. And she feels the board has accomplished some pretty fantastic things.

The woman sitting directly behind them, a manufacturing executive, is listening to the conversation in row 2 as well. She just spent two days at her industry's most important conference, a gathering she attends every year. Once again, the overwhelming majority of speakers at the conference were male, and many of the panels were men-only "manels." When she tracked down the conference's lead organizer and pointed out the lack of women speakers, he told her it's hard to find women who have the expertise to speak at the conference. "How can that be, when every brilliant woman in our industry is a member of your organization?" she asked him. When she started rattling off names, he gave her his business card and told her to email him a list. And then he sided up a little too closely to her and asked her if she wanted to meet for a cocktail that evening. She pushed him away and tore up his business card.

The woman next to her, who works in insurance, feels grateful for *her* CEO as she listens to the guys in row 2. Her CEO doesn't just hire women; he believes in them and supports them. He makes sure she's included in social events, because he knows that they can be as significant a source of information as meetings. When he realizes she's been left out of an important gathering where business is discussed, he briefs her on what she missed. And when the men on her team talk over her in meetings or don't give her airtime, her CEO makes space for her, encourages her participation, directly solicits her opinion, and openly credits her for her ideas. Rather than hoarding power for himself and the men on the team, he shares it with her and the other women executives. Unlike her previous two CEOs, he makes her feel welcome even when she's the only woman in the room.

Fortunately, that happens less often lately because of his efforts to recruit women at every level—more women have been joining the company as word of her CEO's supportiveness spreads. Hmmm, she thinks to herself. Maybe 2A's COO is coming to our company.

As the plane takes off, the CEOs in row 2 give up on trying to figure out how to keep more women in their executive ranks. "That's why we've got HR and a CDO," 2A says, washing his hands of it. "Their problem, I guess. Hey, did you see that game on Sunday?"

Risky Business

Do the challenges facing the guys in row 2 resonate with you? Are you having trouble attracting and retaining female employees? Are you struggling to recalibrate your organization to be more inclusive, to get your workers to adopt the mindsets and behaviors that make diversity possible? Maybe, like those gentlemen, you're tempted just to pour yourself a drink, talk about football, and let the people under you try to deal with it. If so, you and your company are at risk. As other organizations make progress, your company could be left behind, straining to grow and stay relevant while gender-balanced, inclusive companies blow past you in growth. And if your organization falls behind, you may find yourself out of a job.

Making companies more gender-balanced is a sound business decision that provides a range of benefits referred to as "diversity dividends." As the CEO in 2B knows, by just about any measure, introducing greater gender diversity (and other types of diversity as well) creates measurable dividends for the organization in a range of ways. Compared to homogenous organizations, diverse companies have better financial performance, greater innovation, improved insights into customer behavior, and happier employees—both women and men—who stay in their jobs longer.

When leaders and organizations prioritize gender diversity, everyone can benefit. Women have the potential to earn more, feel more comfortable at work, and contribute to their companies in meaningful ways. Businesses can boost productivity and earnings, and connect better with their employees and their customers. And men can have greater access to some of the quality-of-life benefits that so many of them crave. It really is a win-win solution for everyone involved.

But here's what so many people—including the guys in row 2—don't understand about gender balance in the workforce. When it comes to diversity, it's not enough just to go through the motions, no matter how well-intentioned you may be. Installing a chief diversity officer, directing the HR department to recruit women, and getting a certain number of attendees at bias training sessions are all great first starts. But leaders must do more than that. If you just keep doing the same things over and over, you're just dealing with surface issues and not addressing the true root of the problem.

Creating a diverse workplace that delivers all the bottom-line benefits that researchers have identified in gender-balanced organizations is not just about changing behaviors. It's about changing the biased belief systems that permeate our culture. And it's also about creating a corporate atmosphere in which all employees—female and male, white and people of color, straight and LGBTQ—can be their authentic selves. When people at every level feel free to be real, they can do their best work, be their most creative, and drive organizations to the greatest level of success.

Recognizing Biased Belief Systems

Why, when there are so many good reasons to do so, aren't more organizations creating gender balance within their ranks? Why are so many companies still profoundly clueless when it comes to understanding their female employees and their female customers?

Because of a powerful force known as gender bias.

Gender bias exists because of the insidious belief that men are dominant, and women are subordinate. This outdated thinking comes from a belief system known as the male hegemonic power myth, which legitimizes the subordination of women because of the view that they simply aren't as valuable as men in society or in the workplace. (The word hegemony means "dominance.") This belief system creates a gender bias that is wired into us all and is reinforced throughout our lives.

The male hegemonic power myth is a brick wall that holds bias in place and prevents organizations—even those that are trying to do the right thing—from becoming more equitable. This intractable belief system is an 8,000-year-old structure that gives power and dominance to men and takes it away from women. Here's a perfect nutshell-description of what it looks like, from the brilliant Michael Kaufman, PhD, a gender equality researcher and author of *The Time Has Come: Why Men Must Join the Gender Equality Revolution*: "Girls and women denied an education. Denied the vote. Denied a place of authority in our religions. Up against barriers in the workplace. They were expected to have sole responsibility for the never-ending tasks of housework and child rearing. Far too many were silenced by violence."[2]

The male hegemonic power myth upholds rigid definitions of what it is to be a man, and what it is to be a woman. It pushes both genders into rigid roles that are defined not by individual choice, but by a power dynamic that favors men over women from birth to death and biases men against women (and sometimes, against other men who are considered less masculine). Those who try to break out of the roles and power levels imposed on them face punishment ranging from loss of identity to isolation, ostracism, and violence.

Male hegemonic power traps women in obvious ways, but it also traps men. It requires men to see power as their identity, whether they want to or not. It demands that they prove their power constantly as a way to demonstrate that they're more powerful than others, especially women. When a man whose life is ruled by the dictates of male hegemony loses his power, he loses his identity. The fear of losing power can make a man who buys into this mindset desperate to display his power and maintain the status quo. It drives relatively benign actions such as mansplaining and manspreading. It may prevent a man from taking paternity leave. Certainly, it plays a role in the gender pay gap in the United States, where women earn only 80 cents for every dollar paid to men.[3] And in its ugliest and most extreme form, it can drive men to engage in actions such as bullying, discrimination, sexual assault, or even suicide after losing a job that bestowed power and identity.

Rather than being ruled by ineffective and out-of-date male power belief systems, this book guides you to lead with a dignity, which I define as the belief that everyone in an organization has the same worth and the same fundamental human needs as everyone else. Having a Dignity Mindset means you look at every person, every interaction, and every decision with your commitment to dignity set firmly in the front of your mind. When your leadership aligns with the values of a Dignity Mindset, you discard the belief that men are superior; instead, you operate under the belief that everyone in your organization has the same worth and the same fundamental needs as everyone else.

Haven't We Fixed This Already?

You may be thinking that the male hegemonic power myth doesn't really exist anymore. Some women hold top-level jobs, and some men choose to be stay-at-home dads. Women work and men cook dinner. More women than men (56% vs. 44%) attend college.[4] Haven't we come a long way, baby?

Yes, we have made progress. There are many examples of women and men breaking out of the rigid restrictions of male hegemonic power. But we still have a very long way to go. Demonstrations of hegemonic masculinity are often less overt, but they still occur every day, as every woman knows (and as any man who listens to women knows).

As a person, you want to be concerned about the male hegemonic power myth because it's the force behind so many actions that harm both women and men. But as a business leader, you want to be concerned about the fact that male hegemony and the bias it creates has the potential to cripple your organization's success.

Because of bias fueled by the male hegemonic power myth, gender balance (and the dividends it provides) simply isn't happening in corporate America, especially in the executive ranks. Consider this:

- In 2018, only 24 of the CEOs of Fortune 500 companies were women—that's a measly 4.8%.[5]
- That same year, only 21.2% of board seats at S&P 500 companies were held by women.[6]
- If steps aren't taken to add more women to corporate boards, it could take another two generations for the gender balance in boardrooms to match that of the workforce.[7]

- Approximately 42% of women in the United States say they have faced discrimination on the job because of their gender.[8]
- Some 22 to 35% of women report that they have been sexually harassed at work.[9]

Make no mistake: This is not what gender equity in the workplace looks like. We still have a very, very long way to go.

Intentional Change

But despite all this, we have reason to be optimistic. We *can* start to change the biased behaviors that result from hegemonic male mindsets. But first, we must begin to transform the male power belief system that underlies these behaviors. Businesses and leaders that are trying to become more diverse are being undermined on a daily basis by gender bias that exists in our culture at large, as well as in many, but not all, of the men who inhabit the core power structure in our organizations.

Gender bias is so ingrained in our culture that even a lot of well-intentioned men—and some women—are influenced by it. Even those who are trying very hard to bring about change, people who operate under a thoughtfully cultivated gender value system and who try every day to walk the talk on diversity, don't necessarily see how gender bias can cast a shadow over their leadership choices. But we can start to change that, simply by opening our eyes and ears.

It comes down to this: In order for us to solve the gender balance problems in our organizations, we have to shift our view in an entirely new way so that we can see—really see—how gender bias influences us, our organizations, and our society. It's there, and if you think it's not, you've got your head in the sand. Gender bias fueled by male hegemony is so universal and so pervasive that it is often as invisible as the air we breathe. The male hegemonic power myth is so entrenched and ingrained that without looking very hard, you can't even see it. And unless you see it, you can't change it. You can't unlearn it, and you can't lead your organization to unlearn it. As Gloria Steinem says, before we can learn new ways, we must unlearn old ways.

The good news is that once you become aware of the fact that gender bias exists even in situations in which it seems not to, you can start to see it and understand it. Acknowledging its insidiousness can allow you to step outside of it and start to examine and measure it. It's a little like birdwatching: Once you identify it, which we do in this book, you'll start to see it everywhere and wonder how you missed it before. You're already more aware of it simply by virtue of reading this chapter.

When you really see and understand the tremendous impact that gender bias and the male hegemonic power myth has on you, your employees (male and female), and your organization's belief systems, you can start to change those belief systems. Do that, and behavior change will start to happen on its own. The goals that the CEOs in seats 2A and 2B are struggling so hard to achieve—attracting and hiring more women, making them feel welcome, creating an atmosphere in which they can flourish and move your company forward—will happen organically.

Clearing Space for Self-Actualization

When belief systems start to transform and gender bias begins to disappear, you can make space in your organization for a culture that supports self-actualization among all of the people you bring on board to work at your company. Your employees will bloom.

Self-actualization is a phrase you may have learned in a college psychology class. Basically, it is the ability to fulfill your potential and use your talents in a creative, satisfying way. Self-actualization is a basic human need, nearly as powerful as the need for food, water, safety, and love.

How do you support gender-balanced self-actualization? Here's one view. Instead of thinking, "How can we get and keep talented women at our company?" go a step further and ask, "How can we get and keep talented women at our company, and *ensure they are self-actualized in their work?*" Chances are that one reason 2A's COO is leaving his company—why she feels unwelcome even though the organization has made some attempts at gender-balancing behaviors—is that she can't be her true self at work. She landed a top job, but she may not have felt that she could fire on all cylinders once she started showing up for work.

Most women who quit top positions cite the inability to be authentic as the reason for leaving their company. They find that they are working in an impermeable closed shop run by men, and that the only way for them to succeed is to try to function like men. They don't want to do that, because it requires them to pretend to be someone they're not—a little like forcing a right-handed person to write with her left hand. They feel constrained by the doubts projected toward them by men and the ones that they've unconsciously internalized against themselves as a result of living their lives in the male hegemonic power myth. Those are a lot of doubts to face. And consider this: While the woman in the conference room is fighting all these battles while trying to contribute to the discussion, and she's up against a bunch of men whose minds are focused only on their performance, it's hard for the woman to come out ahead. She's fighting with one hand tied behind her back.

Here's a way to visualize this. Anne Jardim is one of the two founding deans of the Simmons University School of Management, where I earned my MBA. She used to talk about something that she referred to as "rings of difference" in an organization, which means that for every *difference* there's a *distance*. If you're a straight white man in an organization, you're at the center of the power structure. But every difference you have— you're a woman, you're a person of color, you're LGBTQ, and so on—puts you at a distance from the power. For every one of those differences, you're pushed a further distance away toward the margins. Every time you want to take an action—whether it's to go for a promotion, volunteer to take on a project, or propose an idea at a meeting—you have to travel through the rings of difference that distance you from power. You have to use up an enormous amount of your creative energy just to attempt to move yourself to a place in which you can start to compete with the straight white men in the room. How exhausting. It reminds me of the quote about the amazing Hollywood dancers Ginger Rogers and Fred Astaire—she did everything he did, except backwards and in high heels. That's what anyone who's not a straight white man in the core power structure has to do.

When you honor the different perspectives that women, people of color, and LGBTQ people bring to the conference table, you make space for these people to be fully authentic, to inhabit their true selves rather than to pretend to be straight white men. (And incidentally, you create a better working environment for men, too.) When people can act authentically, they thrive. They have their best ideas and they feel free enough to share those ideas. They come up with innovative solutions. They feel comfortable enough to contribute the half-baked ideas that, after undergoing the process of supportive brainstorming in a high-trust situation, become fully realized ideas that are so much stronger than what any individuals in the room could have come up with on their own.

A Low-Risk Game

When women don't have the freedom to be authentic, and when they don't trust their team enough to take risks and open up, they often choose to play a low-risk game, holding back on ideas and contributing only when they can do so without repercussions. Or, when they hear about another organization that makes women feel more welcome, they jump ship, as 2A's COO did.

I talk about self-actualization at nearly every women's workshop I lead, and women relate to it vigorously. Their male CEOs just don't realize what it's like to be the outsider in the room, and to have to focus so much of their energy on the daily navigation of figuring out how to fit in, when to speak up, when to stay silent, and when to challenge a man on the team who's speaking over them or ignoring their input. And every now and then one of them—one of the lucky ones—talks about how her CEO creates a climate in which diverse ideas, experiences, opinions, and perspectives are not only welcomed, but are integrated into idea generation and problem solving. Not surprisingly, those women tend to work for companies with significant growth in market share and profits. Those are the companies where other women want to work.

How can we create spaces in our organizations that foster self-actualization and neutralize the rings of difference that interfere with individual and organizational success? As the prosecco-sipping director on the plane can tell you, one of the best ways to design an atmosphere that fosters self-actualization in women is to put them on teams with other women. Take corporate boards, for example. In 2018, only one-third of the boards of Fortune 500 companies had at least three women directors.[10]

Why does that matter? Because one woman on a board or team is a token, and two women can be pushed to the margin by a room full of men. But when there are three women on a board, they are more likely to have the space to self-actualize. It makes room for their points of view, which they are much more likely to share when they're not the only woman on the board.

This isn't just about making women happy. It's about money and corporate success, too. Research has found that having three women on a corporate board represents a tipping point in terms of influence that's reflected in an organization's financial performance.[11] According to MSCI, companies with at least three women on the board saw median gains of 10 percentage points in return on equity (ROE) and 37% in earnings per share (EPS).[12] And companies with no female directors experienced median changes of negative 1 percentage point in ROE and negative 8 percentage points in EPS over the study period. That's pretty dramatic, one could say. Or, one could say, a board that isn't truly diverse (at least three women, as a start), is failing its responsibility to shareholders.

Fear of Power Sharing

Giving power to women in an organization may seem threatening. Let's look at that. If you're a man and you're worried that sharing power with women will reduce your power, you're falling into a trap created by the male hegemonic power myth.

Many leaders have the mentality of scarcity—they're afraid to give up any power because they worry, either consciously or unconsciously, that relinquishing some power would take away from them and reduce their identity. But in reality, the opposite is true, as most successful leaders know. Rather than clinging to the scarcity mentality, embracing the abundance mindset benefits you and your organization because it allows overall power to grow, elevating everyone. Believing in scarcity narrows your thinking and makes you focus on what you lack, but assuming abundance opens your view and allows you to focus on possibilities and potential that lead to growth.

When men choose to lead with the spirit of abundance, they share their power with women in a way that allows the women to flourish and that enhances the performance of everyone on the team—including the men.

The best leaders believe that a candle loses nothing by lighting another candle. When you recognize the negative impact of the male hegemonic power myth, confront bias in your organization, and create pathways for power-sharing and self-actualization among the women, you have the potential to create a blaze of success for everyone in your organization.

Coming Up Next

One of the reasons that the male hegemonic power myth is so difficult to recognize is that all of us—male and female—are steeped in it beginning in infancy. It's cemented in place by the age of 10 and reinforced repeatedly during high school, college, and early employment. By the time men and women come knocking at your door looking for a job, gender bias is so much a part of them that trying to help them unlearn it can seem as difficult as attempting to unscramble an egg.

Fortunately, you can address bias, guide your organization to unlearn destructive gender-bias beliefs, and lead your team to replace bias with positive, unbiased principles that support gender equity. In other words, you can learn how to operate in alignment with Dignity Mindset values. Having a very clear understanding of what the male hegemonic belief system is, where it comes from, and how it permeates our culture can kickstart the unlearning/learning process.

A very wise woman in Birmingham, Alabama, told me recently that you have to take off your own shoes before you can step into someone else's. That's what we'll do in Chapter 2.

CHAPTER 2

Where Gender Bias Begins

"There is a global set of forces from schools, parents, media, and peers themselves that reinforce the hegemonic myths that girls are vulnerable and that boys are strong and independent."

— Robert W. Blum, Kristin Mmari, and Caroline Moreau, Johns Hopkins Bloomberg School of Public Health

While I was on the road recently, a workshop participant shared a story about her 10-yearold daughter. Let's call the girl "Emma." Confident and self-assured, Emma had always been a shining star who felt comfortable expressing her vibrant personality. Emma loved being in the spotlight, performing without hesitation at dances and recitals. For Halloween she dressed as Wonder Woman—the most popular costume of 2017 for girls—and in fourth grade, she ran a winning campaign for the head of the Junior Tech Club that left her parents wondering whether Emma might reshape Silicon Valley one day.

Then, around fifth grade, Emma started to change. Her confidence began to waver, and she showed less interest in being the center of attention. When her mother asked if she planned to run for the Tech Club again, Emma shrugged her shoulders and said no, she just didn't feel like doing it again.

"I don't care if she runs for Tech Club," Emma's dad said. "What worries me is that she seems to be questioning herself in a way that she never has before. I keep wondering, what the hell is happening to my little girl?"

Here's what likely had happened to Emma: Despite her parents' efforts to shield her from the gender norm expectations that they'd both grown up with, Emma had internalized them anyway. Around fifth grade, the oppressive messages of male dominance and female subjugation became too much for her to resist. Like many other girls her age, Emma had absorbed those messages and had reached a tipping point. The weight of male power had become heavy enough to start crushing her down.

Emma was right on schedule. Unfortunately, what occurred to her happens to girls throughout the United States and across the world. Gender bias begins at birth—and even before birth, as anyone who's attended a ballerina girl/football boy-themed baby shower knows. It percolates along during childhood. And then, at around age 10, it erupts and becomes cemented into place not just for girls, but for boys, too.

This origin story is crucial for you to understand as a business leader because the experiences of childhood, adolescence, and early adulthood shape every individual—male and female—who comes to work for you and your organization. A critical part of examining toxic gender belief systems is understanding where they come from. Operating with a Dignity Mindset requires you and all of today's leaders to guide employees to recognize and unlearn the gender mythology with which they grew up.

Let's take a closer look at that mythology.

Gender Norms Across Culture

A wealth of research supports the understanding that the gender bias that permeates children's lives becomes cemented around age 10. Some of the most compelling evidence comes from researchers in the Department of Population, Family, and Reproductive Health at Johns Hopkins Bloomberg School of Public Health. Their watershed study, "It Begins at 10: How Gender Expectations Shape Early Adolescence Around the World," was published in October 2017 in the *Journal of Adolescent Health*.[13] The study looked at groups in 15 countries on five continents: Ecuador, Bolivia, Belgium, Scotland, the United States, South Africa, Malawi, Kenya, DR Congo, Burkina Faso, Nigeria, Egypt, Vietnam, China, and India.

In this study, researchers explored how and when gender norms, or rules, develop across different cultures. They found that throughout the world, the onset of puberty is a major milestone when adults set rigid gender-based rules and mindsets for how girls and boys are to be thought of and how they should behave. The norms about male and female roles permeate children's experiences starting from birth, of course. But the clamps really come on as puberty dawns.

"There is a global set of forces from schools, parents, media, and peers themselves that reinforce the hegemonic myths that girls are vulnerable and that boys are strong and independent. Even in sites where parents acknowledged the vulnerability of their sons, they focus on protecting their daughters," the researchers wrote. Further, the messaging to girls starting around age 10 is that they are the embodiment of sex and sexuality. "Around the world pubertal boys are viewed as predators and girls as potential targets and victims. Messages such as—do not sit like that, do not wear that, do not talk to him, boys will ruin your future—support the gender division of power ... and promote sex segregation to preserve girls' sexuality."

These beliefs about gender norms have a significant impact on both girls and boys, the researchers found. For girls, consequences include an early end to education, as well as child marriage, pregnancy, exposure to violence and sexually transmitted infections, and depression. But boys are also harmed by these male hegemonic beliefs, which lead to engaging in and becoming victims of physical violence, early death from unintentional injuries, substance abuse, and suicide. As children develop into adults, this belief system follows them, infiltrating every part of their consciousness, eventually becoming an unconscious bias that's bad for boys and men, but worse for girls and women.

The Damage of the Male Power Belief System

Achieving gender equity in business won't happen until everyone in that ecosystem truly understands the pervasive, underlying, deeply held belief systems that produce the full range of ugly, subjugating attitudes and behaviors toward women. But, like the Johns Hopkins researchers, I believe that we have the ability to change these damaging belief systems and the behaviors they foster. By investing in understanding the hegemonic male power myth's influence on women's worldviews and everyday life and how that differs from yours (if you're a man), you can facilitate change and build an organization that has more talented women contributing their ideas, gifts, and energy to your teams and customers.

Let's look a little more closely at the male hegemonic power myth. A myth is a widely held but completely false belief. And hegemony is the domination of one group over another. The male hegemonic power myth says the dominating group—men—*deserves* all the power and that they are uniquely capable of commanding, as the Greek root conveys. It says: *This is the way it is supposed to be. Men are more powerful, more worthy than women. And women deserve to be subjugated.*

This myth has been widely propagated through centuries of retelling by the men in power—the men who benefit from it and who want it to stay that way. In every city and town from one side of the world to the other, women suffer from this myth. They are subjugated in a long list of ways because of the belief that men are entitled to dominate them, through any means necessary.

Women are sexualized, tokenized, violated, trafficked, ignored, sexually mutilated, stoned to death *as punishment for being raped*, disfigured, blinded and killed by acid attacks, molested as young girls—often by close male relatives—shamed online for every aspect of their looks and beliefs and self-expression, and driven to suicide by relentless online terror campaigns conducted without consequence across social media. All of these are forms of human torture, and all exist to prop up the male hegemonic power myth. They're also used to perpetuate imbalanced racial power, as readers whose ancestors were seized as slaves understand so very deeply.

We see examples of gender-based violence across the world. In China, women are a driving force of the country's surge in the global economy; and yet, many women in China who earn PhD degrees are subject to gender-based criticism and ridicule—so much so that some people in China joke that the country has three genders: men, women, and the "sexless third gender" of women PhDs who have been branded as "the country's next generation of spinsters."[14] And in Costa Rica, incest levels are so high that reports say 95 percent of pregnant girls under the age of 15 are incest victims."[15] (It's important to point out here that the terrible tragedy of incest exists in all countries including the United States, although incest rates in the U.S. aren't carefully tracked.) I mention Cost Rica here because that country has publicly named this problem and is working to end it, unlike most other countries. In Costa Rica and around the world, the male power myth drives men to express their own power and subjugate women—even their own daughters, granddaughters, and nieces—though sexual assault.

These things don't just happen in other countries—and they happen to boys as well as girls, especially boys who other men perceive to be lower on the male power hierarchy because they're not considered male enough. Here in the United States, 1 in 5 girls and 1 in 20 boys is a victim of sexual abuse; 28% of teens age 14 to 17 have been sexually victimized, often by someone they knew well.[16]

They also happen in the U.S. workplace, where the male power belief system is alive and well. Some of the ways in which it manifests occur when women:

- Are criticized for being too aggressive at work even when they're behaving no differently than their male peers.
- Receive suggestive emails from male co-workers and are told they're "frigid" when they complain.
- Are paid 80 cents for every dollar a man makes. Women of color have an even larger pay gap: black women earn 61 cents for every dollar a man makes, and Latinx women receive 53 cents for a man's dollar.[17] It's interesting to note that the gender wage gap starts in childhood. According to 2018 data collected and analyzed by BusyKid, a mobile app and web platform, girls spend more time on household chores than boys but are paid significantly less for their work, earning an average of $6.71 per week compared with $13.80 per week for boys.[18] BusyKid also found that boys receive more opportunities to earn money than girls, and they save and spend more money for themselves, whereas girls donate more money to charity.
- Are subject to sexual harassment; 22 to 35% of women report that they have been sexually harassed at work.[19]
- Fail to receive promotions when less-qualified men are promoted over them.

- ♦ Are left in the dark about meetings and opportunities to advance.
- ♦ Are fired, demoted, or otherwise penalized spurning the sexual advances of a male boss.

Internalized Oppression

Gender bias against women—from harassment and violence to the full range of gender bias behaviors in today's workplace—exists now because for thousands of years, men have used it to show women who's boss. The male hegemonic power myth upholds rigid definitions of what it is to be a man, and what it is to be a woman. It pushes both genders into strict roles. It tells men that their identity is based on dominating women, and it tells women that they have less value than men.

The Johns Hopkins researchers I mentioned earlier in the chapter discovered that children internalize the gender norms that are forced upon them. Incredibly, they discovered that in some cases, "girls come to internalize these norms to even a greater extent than boys" even though the norms are far more detrimental to women than men. I would venture that this is what happened with Emma, the little girl who decided not to run for Tech Club president again; it's a fair bet that she had absorbed the restrictive male dominance/female subjugation messages from our culture even while being raised by parents who tried valiantly to protect her from them.

The idea that girls internalize harmful gender norms to a greater extent than do boys is a line we can trace all the way from its origins to the truly gifted, talented, high-performing and high-potential women we see in today's organizations who struggle with and are sometimes tortured by confidence issues. Those issues develop at a very young age, in a social system telling girls that they're less than valuable than boys and, on some level, must fear boys. Moms and dads—those who, like Emma's parents, have rigorously taught gender equality through words and actions in their households—notice their daughters start questioning the "you can do and be anything you want!" messaging they grew up with. At around age 10, many girls start to seem lost, more quiet, unsure, and off-balance. These are clear signs that the male hegemonic power myth is getting hold of them.

Don't believe it? If you have a daughter that age, do some sleuthing about what is said on the school bus, one of the most deeply damaging places in childhood, especially for girls. Ask about bullies. Ask about language. Ask if the boys taunt the girls. Ask about sexual references about kids on the bus—about her, even. These actions assault girls' confidence and lay down grooves in their brains and psyches that become deeper and deeper over time.

A decrease in confidence isn't the only collateral damage that starts occurring in girls subjected to the demoralization of the male hegemonic power myth. Importantly, more than a handful of men in any workshop I run will report their own issues with confidence, and this traces back to the same issues: not fitting in with the brand of masculinity that is laid out for them and therefore feeling unsure of their footing at work. It can also affect their learning. Research cited in a 2015 McKinsey report[20] found that gaps in mathematics performance are highest in countries with the greatest levels of gender inequality, and they disappear in countries in which genders are most equal. In Iceland, which has one of the highest levels of gender equality, *females actually outperform males in math*. Female students have lower math scores only in societies in which conventional beliefs hold that men have more value than women, a thought bizarrely linked to the belief that women can't do math and that women are believed to be less valuable than men.

Strong and In Control

During childhood and adolescence, boys learn that they are always supposed to be strong, fearless, and in control. These are ideals that no man can live up to, of course, but that's not what boys hear—the message they receive is that they're supposed to grow into all-powerful men who dominate in every situation. One of the many downsides of this belief is that in situations in which boys can't be strong, fearless, and in control—or worse, when a girl performs better on a test, in a sport, or in any kind of competition—boys may feel defeated, angry, and lost. And in too many situations, the way boys attempt to escape those feelings of inadequacy is to reconnect with aggressive male identity expectations through violence, taunting, or other intimidation and shaming against girls.

In elementary, middle, and high school, the threat of gender-based violence is very real to girls. They face the risk of sexual harassment, sexual assault, and physical assault, as well as the fear of school-based mass shootings, which are almost always committed by boys. Gender-based violence often stems from the power conflicts: When boys see aggression and dominance as part of their identity, they may express this identity by inflicting aggressive, dominant behavior against girls.

Childhood and, especially, adolescence, can be difficult times for kids as they seek to learn their roles in society. Gender bias, peer pressure, and the developmentally normal impulsiveness that exists in the teen brain are a toxic mix that too often leads to violence against girls in school.

Many parents—both moms and dads—teach their kids and reinforce with their daughters that "you can be anyone and do anything you want to in life!" And they do a great job—their daughters believe them. Until they really start experiencing the world for themselves.

As girls internalize female subjugation messages, boys are steeped in assumptions of male power and dominance. Sometimes this occurs subliminally, but it's often quite overt. To see this, look no further than high school sports. Even today, when they should know better, many coaches inflict damage on boys that they carry for life, reinforcing gender bias so effectively that many coaches could serve as poster boys for the male hegemonic belief system. Boys hear comments like this on a daily basis: "You ran down the field like a girl! You're a p---y! Why don't you go join the girls' team, you loser!" If your child plays sports, you might want to check your coaches' attitudes on gender. Some are enlightened, but many are not. There's a lot of shaming that goes on in school sports and most often it's accomplished by telling a boy he acts like a girl, in front of his teammates, and in a way that induces shame. Ask your son. You may be surprised what you hear.

And as a business leader, don't be surprised when you realize that the messages boys hear from their coaches are still running through their heads when they are men working in organizations like yours. Few boys grow up to play for the NFL or the NBA or MLB, but most get jobs, and when they do, they bring that learned gender bias with them when they come to organizations like yours. By then, gender bias and false paradigms are baked into them. Their self-esteem is built on a foundation of a dominant male/

subservient female power dynamic. They pay more attention to the men on their teams than the women. They give more weight to what male colleagues say than female colleagues. And what happens to your business? It loses crucial creativity, problem-solving, ideas, innovation, and competitive advantage because the women don't have a chance to offer them, either because they're not heard or because they're not even in the room to speak because they have already left.

Coming Up Next

When you're bringing women and men into your organization, you're hiring adults, of course. But the beliefs they carry have existed within them since childhood and influence them to this day. The woman on your management team who hesitates to speak up in a meeting may have within her the little girl who was taunted and bullied and frightened on the school bus by boys. The man who talks over her may have within him the boy whose coach demanded that he "man up" and stop playing like a girl. Understanding this is the first step toward changing it.

Your employees' beliefs and behaviors are also influenced by a framing experience known as the "male gaze." It impacts the way that men look at women, women look at themselves, and we all view women in the workplace. In the next chapter we'll take a close look at the male gaze and its impact on organizations.

CHAPTER 3

How the Male Gaze Curates Our Worldview

"As long as she thinks of a man, nobody objects to a woman thinking."

— Virginia Woolf

You're on a long-haul flight across the United States, feeling lucky that you're on a plane that actually has screens. Sure, you should be working on that report that's due tomorrow, but what you really feel like doing is relaxing, headphones on, watching a good movie. You put in your ear buds, recline your seat, and check out your list of movie choices:

A Wrinkle in Time	*Tully*
Ocean's 8	*Book Club*
Mama Mia! Here We Go Again	*Peppermint*
On the Basis of Sex	*Colette*
RBG	*The Color Purple*
Can You Ever Forgive Me?	*Tiny Furniture*
A Simple Favor	*The Passion of Joan of Arc*
The Hate U Give	*Claudine*
Eighth Grade	*Love with The Proper Stranger*
Captain Marvel	*Mahogany*
Wonder Woman	*Frances Ha*
Nobody's Fool	*Bridesmaids*
The Spy Who Dumped Me	

That's quite a line-up of choices isn't it? A nice selection of recent hits and old favorites.

Now, go back and look at the list again. Does anything jump out at you as you scan it?

If you noticed that all of these films prominently feature women actors and have plots focusing on female characters and their stories, you're right. And bonus points to you if you observe that these films have all made boatloads of money.

Here's the thing, though: You would never, ever see this list of movies on a commercial airline. You'd probably never see it anywhere, except maybe at a women's film festival. Instead, your in-flight movie list would look more like the one I saw recently on a cross-country flight:

Avengers: Infinity War
Mission: Impossible—Fallout
Ant-Man and the Wasp
Deadpool 2
Aquaman
Spider-Man: Into the Spider-Verse
First Man
Solo: A Star Wars Story
Blindspotting
BlacKkKlansman
Overlord
Vice
Green Book
Venom
Bohemian Rhapsody
The Mule
Incredibles 2
Isle of Dogs

Okay, I'm going to stop there because the real list goes on and on and on, and I think you get my point. The movie choices on my recent flight included one movie after another featuring male characters and overwhelmingly male-centric plots. The women in most of these movies tend to be accessories, playing supporting roles of wives, girlfriends, or female co-workers whose breasts get more screen time than their faces. Either that, or they're venomous bosses or sexy bad girls attempting to stand between the male protagonists and their goals. These female characters may not even have names; their function is only to advance the story for the men in the film.

If a male passenger on your flight saw that first list, with all those female stars and stories, he'd probably wonder what the heck was going on. Why would the airline be playing all those women's films? Where were the "mainstream" movies? Most likely he'd look around and wonder if he'd accidentally boarded a charter flight of women en route to a women-only event. "These movies aren't for me; I feel I don't belong here," he'd almost certainly say to himself. And yet, when a woman is offered choices like those on the second list, she's expected to feel satisfied. For women, this is standard operating procedure. When I say that male dominance and female subordinance is in the very air we breathe, this is the kind of thing I'm talking about.

Here's what happens every time passengers settle in to choose a movie from a curated list on a flight. Men receive options that cater to their needs, desires, and preferences. And women? They too receive options that cater to men's needs, desires, and preferences. Nobody would expect men to choose from a selection of movies that overwhelmingly focus on women and their stories. But women are expected to get excited about yet another *Mission: Impossible* movie in which Tom Cruise saves the day while a gorgeous woman lingers just behind his shoulder gazing up at him— always *up*, even though Tom Cruise is shorter than many of his female co-stars—adoringly, lovingly, helplessly, fetchingly supporting his domination while she subjugates her own strengths and identity.

That's the "male gaze." It's the viewpoint that sees nearly everything— cinema, art, literature, business, sports, medicine, psychology, philosophy, history, and just about everything else in the world, including women—from the male perspective. From the frame of the male gaze, women exist only for the enjoyment and service of the male spectator. From the viewpoint of the male gaze, men are always the main characters, and women only play supporting roles. With this perspective women are always the "other."

Objects of Desire

British film theorist Laura Mulvey first brought the term "male gaze" into the cultural conversation in the 1970s with the publication of her essay, "Visual Pleasure and Narrative Cinema."[21] In her essay, she pointed out that movies (and many other forms of art) frame spectators as masculine while showing women on screen as objects of desire. This male perspective, or male gaze, encourages viewers to identify with male protagonists *even when those viewers are female*. It is a pervasive screen that filters everything we see, wrapping and warping our view of the world.

Mulvey described the male gaze as "the act of depicting the world and women in the visual arts and literature from a masculine and heterosexual point of view, presenting women as *objects* of male pleasure." She went on to say that the imbalance of gender power in movies is not just a minor point; it is a controlling force that is concerned only with creating satisfaction for the male viewer. Women are portrayed as erotic objects both for the characters within the movie, and for the viewing audience—an audience presumed to be straight, white, and male. Male characters are the heroes; females are passive subjects. Patriarchal order is maintained, praised, and positioned as "natural."

The male gaze doesn't just influence the movies we see; indeed, it curates our entire worldview. The male gaze feeds the beast—the male hegemonic power myth—through mass-consumed film and entertainment. What a boost the male gaze gives the power myth! Every film constructed to reinforce the hegemony of male power is like an advertisement that imprints millions and millions of impressions into the minds of young and old alike. Every movie that showcases the male gaze teaches young boys and girls that men matter more than women, that it's a man's job to save the world and a woman's job to boost his ego as he fights and then make love to him as a reward. Successful men who embody the powerful male role "get the girl" in the end, and females become the prize that men receive when they express their male identity. The male gaze reinforces the idea that men are dominant, and women are subordinate, and the male viewpoint is right, best way to look at the world.

Perhaps you've heard of the Bechdel Test. Developed by cartoonist Alison Bechdel, it is a simple measure of the representation of women in fiction and a useful way to help quantify the male gaze. To pass the Bechdel test, a film must meet three criteria: To have (1) two or more named female characters who (2) talk to each other about (3) something other than a man. That's it. Seems like it should be an easy test to pass. And yet, incredibly, only about 58% of U.S. films meet all three criteria in the Bechdel Test.[22] Some of the failures include *Harry Potter and Deathly Hallows: Part II*, *Slumdog Millionaire*, *Moonlight*, *La La Land*, the entire *Lord of the Rings* trilogy, *Toy Story 1* and *2*, *The Avengers*, *Lara Croft: Tomb Raider*, *Avatar*, and *Finding Nemo*.[23]

Although we see the male gaze in popular movies, its existence predates modern cinema by centuries. It has existed since the ancient times of oral tradition, in the written word, in the development of most religions as a way to maintain a worldview that keeps men in power and relegates women to the invisible roles of serving and propping up men. The male gaze in cinema, gaming, and social media are just the latest iterations of propping up the male power myth.

Normalizing the Male Gaze

Over time, the male gaze-reinforced image of the patriarchy as "natural" reaches beyond cinema and entrenches into the wider culture. It is so deeply rooted that it goes unchallenged and seems normal. This creates a false but dominant belief that masculinity is worthy of praise, and femininity's only use is to serve men.

Mulvey included in her essay a call to feminist filmmakers to destroy the patriarchal Hollywood system and create movies that challenge this view. A glance at the movie menu on a long-haul flight shows that we still have a long way to go to achieve Mulvey's goal.

Certainly, Hollywood has made some progress since Mulvey published her essay more than four decades ago. More movies tell stories through a female gaze or a gender-neutral gaze. And women are taking lead roles in the types of films that previously would have featured men. Take superhero movies, for example. *Wonder Woman* (starring Gal Gadot) and *Captain Marvel* (starring Brie Larson) broke new ground culturally and financially.

For example, in its opening weekend alone, Brie Larson's *Captain Marvel* earned $455 million internationally.[24]

And yet, for every step forward we move backward, too. Like other female-focused movies, both *Wonder Woman* and *Captain Marvel* experienced huge backlashes because they featured female superheroes. And despite stunning box office success and positive critical reviews, *Captain Marvel* was the target of an enormous wave of gender-based trolling. The female-debasing reaction against *Captain Marvel* was so intense that the film review site Rotten Tomatoes made major changes to its reviewing rules after it became clear that its reviewers (of whom more than three-quarters are male) were deliberately trying to sabotage the movie before it even opened, all because it features a female superhero. Here is another example of men curating our collective, warped worldview.

If some men get that upset and take that kind of action against women simply because they play a lead role in a superhero movie, imagine how those men react when they show up at work on a Monday morning and discover that they're working for a female CEO. Some, but certainly not all, of these men feel threatened by the thought of sharing power with women. And although it's tempting to write these men off as exceptions—comic book super fans obsessing over the proper Marvel world order—they're not. They're the men you see every day. They're working in your organization, sitting at your conference table, working on teams with the women you hire. They identify with the male hegemonic power myth, and they believe that the male gaze is the only right way to view the world—and your company.

Despite the progress being made to reframe the male gaze, it still exerts an overwhelming influence on our culture. Most of the power in Hollywood remains in male hands, even after #MeToo. In 2019, as in nearly every other year, men received *all* of the Best Director nominations for Academy Awards; since 1929, only five women have been nominated for Best Director and only one, Kathryn Bigelow, has won.[25] The Time's Up and #MeToo movements have shined a spotlight on sexual harassment in the workplace and have created critical awareness about its prevalence, but we still have a long way to go. It's important to note that Tarana Burke, an American social activist and community organizer, founded the MeToo movement in 2006 to raise awareness of sexual abuse and assault in society.

Not only does the male gaze continue to frame our worldview, but women continue to be belittled, ignored, and even assaulted as they look for roles to fill, whether as an actor, a developer, or an end user. The male gaze drives the way we see the world—and women.

Having more movies with women in lead roles can help chip away at the male gaze as the go-to perspective in popular culture. As women and evolved men push for inclusion in roles and plots—not just for women, but for people of color and non-heteronormative individuals—I hope our collective gaze can start to shift away from the male viewpoint.

We know that viewers want this. Research conducted by Creative Artists Agency (CAA) and the tech company shift7 found that movies with women in lead roles have outperformed movies led by men at the box office recently. (The study looked at 350 of the top-grossing films between 2014 and 2017.) That same study found that since 2012, all of the films that made more than $1 billion at the box office have passed the Bechdel Test. As the *Fast Company* article about this research finding points out, this is "a clear signal to Hollywood that inclusion isn't just a fad—it's smart business."[26]

Beyond the Screen

The male gaze doesn't just apply to movies. In the decades since Mulvey identified the male gaze in cinema, the term has come to encompass the screen through which we view nearly every aspect of our world. The male gaze frames the content, narrative, and bias in our world at large and within organizations. It extends to online gaming and social media (which we look at in the next chapter) and influences entities that you might expect to be unbiased.

Here's a look at some other places within our culture that are viewed overwhelmingly through the male gaze.

Wikipedia: When you have a question or need some quick information, you probably check out Wikipedia for answers. Launched in 2001, Wikipedia is among the top sources of information on the internet. Many millennials grew up with it, and most of your employees probably refer to it on a regular basis.

If you think Wikipedia is unbiased in regard to gender, you're wrong. In fact, the online information warehouse's male bias is so extensive that Wikipedia doesn't even try to hide it. Go to Wikipedia, look up "gender bias on Wikipedia," and here is what you'll learn: "A dominant majority of volunteer Wikipedia editors, particularly on the English-language site, are male. This has led to Wikipedia having fewer and less extensive articles about women or topics important to women. It figures among the most frequent criticisms of Wikipedia."[27] In fact, 90% of Wikipedia editors are male.[28]

The entry goes on to say that the Wikimedia Foundation, which runs Wikipedia, agrees with these criticisms and has made an ongoing attempt to increase female editorship of Wikipedia." Credit where credit is due: Wikipedia is to be commended for confronting this head-on. Gender bias within Wikipedia extends beyond its editors to its content subjects: Only about 18% of Wikipedia's biographical articles are about women.[29] This is so huge—it gives a tremendous boost to the male gaze and reinforces why we literally learn not to look for women because we can't see them or find them in extremely important places like Wikipedia, the "world's answer book."

Wikipedia's bias matters because it is yet another example of how the male gaze defines and curates the frame through which women and men (and girls and boys) view our world. When men develop social media platforms and focus the user experience primarily on the needs, viewpoints, interests, and preferences of other men, the perspective is distorted in favor of men and against women. Through this distortion, men create the story (or platform, or exchange), men frame the story (through camera angles, platform functionality, usability), and the woman's role is to buy into it all.

Satellite Radio: Have you ever sat in a car with satellite radio and searched the hundreds of channels for music you'd enjoy? As you flip around, you'll find lots of choices framed by the male gaze. One of the biggest satellite radio stars is Howard Stern, who is possibly the most misogynistic person on the air today. If anti-female smut isn't to your liking, you can also find channels named Frank Sinatra, Pitbull, Elvis, the Beatles, B. B. King, Tom Petty, all the men's professional sports teams from hockey to football to basketball, the Grateful Dead, Joel Osteen, Jeff &

Larry's Comedy Roundup, Kevin Hart, The Garth Channel, and Willie's Roadhouse, to name a few. There are also category channels for gospel and other types of music. So many choices—and yet, as of this writing, not one channel has a woman's name—not music, comedy, sports, or religion.

Don't look for women's names on the Ranker list of "Best DJs in the World Right Now," either, because they're all men.[30] And that's not because only men become DJs. There are plenty of fantastic female DJs, including Monika Kruse, Nora En Pure, Honey Dijon (a transgender DJ), Nina Kraviz, Helena Hauff, Ellen Allien, Nicole Moudaber, Charlotte de Witte, and Gayle San. But you won't find them on that list, because the male gaze doesn't see them. When men do the curation, only the male viewpoint is represented.

If we were to remove the male gaze screen from our eyes and widen our frame to examine just one of these successful artists, Monika Kruse of Germany, here are a few things we'd learn: She's known as "The Queen of Techno" in Europe and is fully booked at the biggest events all year round. Her work spans over two decades, and she formed her own label, Terminal M, in 2001. That year, Kruse formed a social justice organization, No Historical Backspin, a platform for Electronic Artists to make a stand against racism, intolerance, and xenophobia. (And by the way, it was only recently that this talented woman received a bio page on Wikipedia.)

Wall Street: In March 2017 a bronze sculpture known as "Fearless Girl" created by artist Kristen Visbal was installed in the Financial District in Manhattan. The statue was commissioned by State Street Global Advisors, a financial firm based in Boston known for leading the way in advocating gender balance on boards and within organizations. Fearless Girl stood in front of Charging Bull, a Wall Street icon that represents power and resilience in a bear market. SSGA said Fearless Girl, which was unveiled on the eve of International Woman's Day, signified the power of women in leadership[31] and was also a sales promotion for a new index fund focusing on women.

The statue of a young girl in a ponytail, leaning forward with a look of fierce determination in her eyes quickly gained popularity. Many tourists, including lots of women, showed up in droves to have their photos taken with Fearless Girl. The juxtaposition of Fearless Girl and Charging Bull really was breathtaking.

About six weeks after Fearless Girl appeared on the scene, one man, upset with the attention she was attracting, defiled her. He erected a statue that came to be known as Pissing Pug, a clumsily cobbled together scrap of metal in the likeness of a dog urinating on Fearless Girl's leg.[32]

The man who did this expressed intense anger for various reasons about Fearless Girl. The anger that drove him to debase that wonderful, dignified, inspiring image of a young girl ready to take on the world was apparently a triggering event for him. Evolved men who see women as their equal celebrated Fearless Girl's strength, but men whose identities are based on a foundation of male domination and female subjugation likely felt the earth shift beneath them to think of a female—a young girl, no less—getting all that attention in the center of the world's financial power seat. The male gaze wants to focus on a Charging Bull, not a Fearless Girl.

Medical Research: The male gaze even extends into hospitals and medical laboratories. You might think that something as scientific as medical research would escape gender bias, but that's not the case. Astonishingly, medical studies often include only small numbers of women subjects even for conditions such as heart disease, which kills more women than men. That's right: Many of the medical procedures and drugs used to treat women with cardiovascular disease were tested primarily on men—in fact, only one-third of subjects in cardiovascular disease studies are female.

According to a major 2014 report issued by researchers at Harvard teaching hospital Brigham and Women's and The George Washington University, despite some progress over the previous two decades, women still have not achieved equity in biomedical and health outcomes investigations.[33] "The science that informs medicine— including the prevention, diagnosis, and treatment of disease—routinely fails to consider the crucial impact of sex and gender," the report states. "This happens in the earliest stages of research, when females are excluded from animal and human studies or the sex of the animals isn't stated in the published results. Once clinical trials begin, researchers frequently do not enroll adequate numbers of women or, when they do, fail to analyze or report data separately by sex." So much for the objectivity of science.

What does bias in medicine look like? Take heart attacks, for example. Heart attacks in women may be missed—even by emergency room doctors—because their symptoms can present differently than those of men. According to a 2016 report by the American Heart Association, men having a heart attack are more likely to have "typical" symptoms such as chest pain and chest discomfort; and women are more likely to experience "atypical" symptoms such as nausea, dizziness, indigestion, and fatigue.[34] Notice the language used there: The male experience is defined as "typical," and the female experience as "atypical." That tells you something right there. The male gaze curates women's experiences even as they face possible death from heart attack.

The sciences pose another challenge for women. Some of the women who study science in college and graduate school and work hard to get their dream jobs—often in laboratories—may find themselves victims of harassment by men. What's worse, female scientists are reluctant to report this harassment because it could end their careers. "From grad-school admission on up through tenure, every promotion can hinge on a recommendation letter's one key passage of praise, offered—or withheld— by the most recent academic advisor. Given the gender breakdown of senior scientists, most often that adviser is a man," wrote scientist A. Hope Jahren in a 2016 opinion column in the New York Times.[35] "This is central to the answer of why we don't have more women rising in the STEM fields," notes Dr. Deya Corzo, a geneticist and pediatrician working both in industry and as an instructor at Harvard Medical School. "As women in the sciences, we must accept the responsibility to serve as advisors in the largest numbers possible to help our female colleagues find their footing and bring their talents center stage."

Redirecting the Gaze

We all have lenses through which we see the world. These lenses come from various places—gender, family upbringing, formal education, social class—as well as the perspective of the male gaze in popular culture. To help close the gender gap, each of us needs to examine how our own unique screens filter our view of the world. Worldview shapes our belief systems, and belief systems shape how we behave with people who are different than we are.

Identifying our own screen can be difficult, because unless you really look for it, it remains invisible. In the second half of this book, where we focus on making business decisions that align with a Dignity Mindset, we look at tools we can use to help us see our own screens of bias and learn how to remove them, and how to help employees do this, too. In the meantime, becoming aware of the impact and reach of screens such as the male gaze can begin to open your eyes.

Leaders in organizations who want to create truly inclusive environments know the first order of business is to lead the way in removing the screens of prejudice, and to demand that others do so as well. Identifying and starting to dismantle the male gaze screen is a key part in how we can ensure that women are included, seen, valued, developed, and advanced with the same generosity and appreciation that men receive. As a leader, it's crucial for you to understand how the male gaze affects your employees. They are surrounded by it from birth. Children's televisions shows and movies start perpetuating the male perspective from day one—think of Cinderella, who is saved by the prince. From our earliest days, we see vivid examples of powerful men protecting powerless women, and those examples are reinforced throughout our lives.

From birth to the launch of their career, many men have a perspective on women that's framed almost completely by the male gaze. They don't see women as anything but bit characters in their own male story. They talk over them in meetings, they mansplain, and they cluster in their own tight, familiar power-sharing male networks. And the worst among them exercise their male entitlement through assault and rape. When they reach positions of power, too many turn into the Harvey Weinsteins of the world.

Well beyond the movies, there is extensive literature showing how women trying to secure venture capital for their next new idea are encouraged to go through the same terror and torture experienced by women in Hollywood. When it comes to Hollywood and Silicon Valley, the apple doesn't fall far from the tree. In these scenarios, men expect to hold all the power, they believe the women around them exist only for their pleasure, and they expect not to be held accountable for taking that to which they feel they are entitled.

Coming Up Next

After reading this chapter, you should have a solid understanding of how the male gaze in cinema and throughout our culture frames gender-biased worldviews. It's a powerful force, with far-reaching impact. But guess what? The effect it has on women—internalized bias and a sense of lessness—in today's workforce pales in comparison to the influence of gaming and social media. Seriously. You haven't seen anything yet.

In the next chapter, we explore the ways in which video games and social media cement the concept of male power in boys and men. These platforms are insidious because when boys and men play them, they don't just *observe* the male hegemonic power myth in a passive way, as they do with movies and television. Rather, they *embody* it and become captive to it in a way that can overtake their consciousness. Most men you recruit for positions in your organization will have spent thousands and thousands of hours playing and being *active, first-person* participants in physically violent, sexually misogynistic video games that have literally changed the way their brains function.

The next chapter looks at how these experiences impact men in the workplace—not only in terms of gender bias, which is a negative, but in helping them to develop high-level strategic experience, which some women workers may not develop to the same extent because they don't play all those games.

CHAPTER 4

The Male Gaze Goes Digital

"Ask a man what his greatest fear is about serving jail time, and he will almost inevitably say he fears being raped. What can we deduce from the fact that jail is to men what life is to so many women?"

— Soraya Chemaly, author and director of the
Women's Media Center Speech Project

It's Monday morning and you're at your desk interviewing Joe, an impressive young job candidate, for an important position on your team. He has plenty to offer: exceptional experience, near-perfect grades from a top university, and a solid recommendation from a trusted colleague. He presents himself well and is personable, well-spoken, energetic, and super smart.

That's what you know about this seemingly flawless job candidate. But what you don't know is that in his free time, this particular candidate enjoys shooting women in strip clubs, murdering prostitutes after having sex with them, and then taking selfies in front of their lifeless bodies.

No, Joe isn't a psychopathic maniac. He's just a guy who, like millions of others, enjoys playing video games in his free time. There are plenty of people who play video games for fun. The average male spends about seven hours a week gaming.[36] Sometimes he plays at home, to blow off steam after a long day at work. And sometimes he sneaks in some playtime at work. To be sure, some gamers play hours of the extensive Mario Kart series, but Joe's favorite game is Grand Theft Auto, one of the most popular gaming franchises in history.

As a businessperson, you'd be impressed with the success of Grand Theft Auto. Its most recent iteration, Grand Theft Auto V, has sold more than 90 million units since its launch in 2013 and has earned its publisher over $6 billion, making it the most financially successful media title of all time.[37] Version V owes its success in large part to the addition of a first-person point of view, which allows players to experience the game through their own perspective.

The first-person perspective that Grand Theft Auto introduced with version V was a game changer for the franchise, propelling an already successful product into the stratosphere of gaming popularity. Players love the upgrade, because it allows them to feel as if they, rather than the characters in the game, are performing the actions on the screen. That's what Joe likes most about Grand Theft Auto V. When Joe settles in for some gaming fun, *he* drives the car. *He* fights the bad guys. *He* shoots the guns. And *he* enjoys the services of the 3D prostitutes who do whatever he wants to him in the front seat of his car. "Now you can pick up these women and experience them from the comfort of your very own virtual lap," writes a columnist for TheGamer.com, a gaming news site.[38]

It's tempting in discussions like these to vilify men who play video games, but it would be wrong. The message here is *not* that men are bad. Absolutely not. There are a lot of reasonably harmless, wildly entertaining video games on the market today. The purpose here is to build awareness of how some of these games contribute to gender bias and reinforce the belief systems your employees bring with them to work. As a leader, you are trying to engage and align all your employees around key goals, but some of those folks' core beliefs are deeply influenced by their gaming activity.

The GTA V crowd lives with a gender-biased belief system that surrounded them in childhood, was reinforced repeatedly in adolescence, and solidified in young adulthood. If you want to start to reduce gender bias and attract and retain women in your organization—and create a work environment that allows both women and men to perform at their highest possible level—it is crucial for you to have an awareness of how gaming and another powerful digital force, social media, are affecting the people you already employ and the candidates, like Joe, who hope to join your team. Perhaps you are already beginning to see why the context around tactics like adding Employee Resource Groups are a start but how much more is needed to achieve your goals for gender balance and inclusion.

The Gaming Gaze

In the previous chapter we talked about how movies that adopt the male gaze show the world through men's viewpoint, with women filling only secondary roles such as the hero's love interest, wife, mother, sister, boss, or the roadblock standing between him and his goals. Exposure to the male gaze begins during childhood—toddlerhood, even—when kids begin watching movies such as *Cinderella, Sleeping Beauty, Aladdin,* and others that objectify women and reinforce the male power myth. Viewed through the male gaze, women (and girls) exist only for the enjoyment and service of men (and boys). Video games pick up where mainstream cinema leaves off, with some of them amplifying the male gaze to a disturbing extent. Early video games rated for "everyone" are milder fare, but once kids start straying into "teen," "mature 17+," and "adults only 18+" territory, the gaze starts turning toxically male. These games make men the center of the world—a world that, thanks to advances in technology, looks more and more real with every update. Women often (but not always) exist in this very male-centric world only as sexual playthings, the source of jokes, or potential victims of physical or sexual violence. If you haven't taken a look at some of these games it's a good education, though a very sobering one. It is here, within these virtual worlds, that many boys and young men develop their ideas about women and their value, or lack thereof.

Men who enjoy gaming—like our job candidate Joe—would tell you that the messaging in this subset of violent and misogynistic video games doesn't touch them because they know right from wrong and can separate the fantasy behavior of a video game from real-life behavior. That's true to a point—with only a few exceptions, men who drive their cars onto a sidewalk full of pedestrians in a video game simply for the fun of killing them wouldn't do it in in real life, right? But when it comes to behavior toward women, the reality is more complicated than that.

Gaming scenarios that promote the minimalization, devaluing, abuse, torture, and murder of women have a cumulatively numbing effect on boys and men, normalizing the idea of violence against women.

Not 'Just Games'

Men "can say that these are 'just games,' and that they have no impact beyond themselves.

But the attitudes about women, and the roles women have in the world, are influenced by the fantasy that games offer," writes Carolyn Petit, a transgender journalist and gaming writer. "They have this idea that gaming is like a magic circle that they enter, where they enjoy a fantasy, and then they come out of it into the real world without having been influenced at all. It doesn't work like that."[39]

Considering what we know about the human brain, it seems naïve to think that games like these could leave players unaffected. In fact, "scientific research has demonstrated an association between violent video game use and increases in aggressive behavior, aggressive affect, aggressive cognitions, and decreases in prosocial behavior, empathy, and moral engagement," according to the American Psychological Association.[40] Playing video games activates the brain's pleasure circuits, causing the brain to release dopamine and other pleasure-inducing neurochemicals.[41]

For too many gamers, playing becomes an obsession. In 2018, the World Health Organization recognized "gaming disorder" as a medical condition and added it to its International Classification of Diseases (ICD-11).[42] This shouldn't be a surprise, because scientists have found that playing video games not only can impact how the brain performs, but can actually alter the brain's structure, with neural changes that are similar to those that occur in addictive disorders such as alcohol addiction and gambling addiction.[43] According to WHO, people with gaming disorder have trouble controlling the amount of time that they spend playing video games, and they experience detrimental effects as a result of prioritizing gaming over other activities. Medical experts believe it could affect up to 1% of the population. Doesn't that make you wonder about the high schools in at least eight states that have made competitive video game playing a varsity sport?[44]

The way that gaming warps a man's view of women can follow him into work. A man whose world view about men and women is formed with the influence of video games may believe in men as the dominating center of the world (and the office); even if he pays lip service to gender equity, he may not really *believe* in it.

It's easy for men who grow up on a steady diet of misogynistic video games, which fit neatly into the broader cultural male hegemonic power myth, to feel threatened—and angry—when women at work challenge them or present an idea that's better than theirs. Even if they know *in theory* that the women they work with supposedly have the same value as the men, they may not know how to treat women as equal. In a game, they might shoot an assertive woman or run her over with their car. At work, they belittle her idea, speak over her in a meeting, joke with other men about the size of her breasts, or simply ignore her. "Men are told in our society that they should get fast cars and hot women and good jobs," writes Anita Sarkeesian,[45] head of Feminist Frequency, a not-for-profit educational organization that analyzes modern media's relationship to societal issues such as gender, race, and sexuality.[46] "And when they don't get those things, they attack women they perceive as being successful."

One of the most stunning things about these games is that they have been developed without *any* consideration or concern about their impact on the lives of women. This is such an important issue for all of us—especially business leaders—to understand. Consider the fact that the safety and well-being of *half* of the world's population has been completely ignored by biased game developers and users. Why is there so little concern about how today's video games affect women? And men?

When Girls Play

It's not just boys and men who play video games. Some girls and women do, too. However, the messages females take from mainstream video games are quite different than those that males receive. With their strong male gaze, mainstream video games bolster a man's sense of gender identity. He comes away from a video game feeling powerful and dominant—even if he didn't play the game well, he still feels like a winner because he's on the gender team that always comes out ahead. Women, on the other hand, receive the message that, no matter how well they play, they lose because their gender always comes in second to men. Whether or not they're conscious of it, women absorb the dominant male perspective in which women are routinely victimized and conquered because the coder who created the game, from his male gaze, built the female characters as inherently worthless.

When girls play sexist video games, they embody the first-person male perspective, just as men do. This active participation experience chips away at their own belief systems with toxic misogynistic messages about them and their gender. These messages internalize the experience of female oppression, which is consistent with so many other messages girls get from the world around them. These messages imprint on a girl's psyche, contributing to the confidence problems that many girls experience in their teens and, in some cases, carry into adulthood and to their jobs at organizations like yours. If this were not so, how could we explain the rampant epidemic of women at work reporting feeling the negative effect of imposter syndrome and low confidence?

A male executive told me a heartbreaking story about discovering that his 8-yearold daughter had accidentally watched a woman being abused in a video game. He was crushed imagining the damage this experience did to his young child. Images like that can't be un-seen or forgotten, and they may jump into the front of girls' minds in a posttraumatic stress disorder-like way when they are threatened by boys or men. That's right—thanks to the marvels of gaming technology, women can feel the emotional aftereffects of sexual violence even if they've never actually been assaulted.

Keep that in mind when a woman on your team has trouble standing up to a man who's verbally bullying her.

Missed Skills

In an unfortunate irony, some girls and young women who choose not to play video games may be missing out on the development of crucial skills: strategic thinking and planning under pressure. Because of their complexity, performing well in all kinds of video games helps players strengthen their strategic thinking abilities. The repetitive nature of the video game experience allows players to experiment with tactics, learn from mistakes, plan ahead, and experience confidence-boosting rewards for exceptional performance. Video games can teach problem-solving, resourcefulness, and multitasking. These are necessary skills for video game success—and business success. It's no surprise that researchers in the UK found that girls who play video games are three times more likely to pursue a STEM degree than those who don't.[47]

Girls and women who want to protect themselves from the degrading experience of playing misogynistic video games may lose access to this potentially worthwhile skill-building experience. The way to correct this is for game designers to create a much richer inventory of bias-free video games that girls and women can enjoy without selling out their very own agency in the process.

Fortunately, as more female game developers join the industry—although it's still quite heavily male—we can hope to see video games that empower women and help them build strategic thinking and other healthy life skills. And for those women who have no interest in playing video games, there are other less toxic ways to strengthen strategic thinking skills. We'll explore some of these in Part II of this book.

Social Media and Female Confidence

We opened this chapter having you picture yourself on a Monday morning interviewing Joe, a male job candidate whose view of women has been influenced by video games. Now let's shift focus. Today is Tuesday, and you're at your desk interviewing Zoe, an impressive young female job candidate, for an important position on your team. She has plenty to offer: exceptional experience, near-perfect grades from a top university, and a solid recommendation from a trusted colleague. She presents herself well and is personable, well-spoken, energetic, and super smart.

That's what you know about this seemingly flawless job candidate. What you don't know is that she was so nervous before this job interview that she felt nauseous in the Uber on the way to your office. You also don't know that she considered canceling the interview because she figured she wouldn't be qualified enough to get the job anyway, and even if she did receive an offer from you, she might not be able to keep up with all the other talented people on your team.

When you look at Zoe and her resume, you see a highly qualified candidate with stellar accomplishments. But that's not what Zoe sees. Because of a lack of confidence that she's carried with her since middle school, Zoe feels out of place in the interview despite her educational and career success. She has a classic case of imposter syndrome, a well-documented phenomenon that affects too many women who feel they're one step away from being uncovered as a fraud.

Imposter Syndrome

Imposter syndrome was first described in 1978 in an article by Dr. Pauline Rose Clance and Dr. Suzanne Imes at Georgia State University.[48] (They called it "imposter phenomenon," but it's more commonly referred to as "imposter syndrome" today.) In that article, Clance and Imes defined imposter syndrome as an internal experience of intellectual phoniness that appears to be particularly prevalent and intense among a select sample of high achieving women. "Despite outstanding academic and professional accomplishments, women who experience the imposter phenomenon persist in believing that they are really not bright and have fooled anyone who thinks otherwise," the researchers wrote. "Numerous achievements, which one might expect to provide ample object evidence of superior intellectual functioning, do not appear to affect the impostor belief." Unfortunately, that description is as accurate today as it was when they wrote it in 1978.

How prevalent is imposter syndrome? Research suggests that as many as 70% of people will experience at least one episode of imposter syndrome in their lives.[49] (Once in their *lives?* Many women with imposter syndrome would probably say they experience it as least once a *day.*) Go to any seminar or workshop in which women feel comfortable opening up about their workplace worries and you'll find that imposter syndrome—and its close sibling, lack of confidence—is rampant. This isn't scientific, and while some women will never experience lack of confidence, when I ask women in my audiences to raise their hands if imposter syndrome is a problem for them, I'd say between 70-90% say yes, even if not every day. Although imposter syndrome primarily strikes women, it affects men, also—including, but not limited to, gay men and men of color.

Social Media and Confidence

Imposter syndrome has many drivers. First and foremost is the internalization by girls and young women of the sex-role stereotypes enforced by the male hegemonic power myth. Clance and Imes identified other contributors as well, including family dynamics and culture. But today there exists an imposter syndrome driver that researchers could never have foreseen in the late 1970s: social media.

For all the hours job candidate Joe spends playing video games, job candidate Zoe spends a similar amount of time on social media. And, although social media is certainly less overtly harmful to women (and men), its negative impact on women in the workplace can be almost as insidious because it can eat away at their confidence and self-esteem. Social media tells girls that everyone else is prettier, happier, thinner, smarter, and more successful than they are; it creates a world in which everything a girl does is put up to a popularity vote. Important thoughts and experiences have the potential to lose value when they don't get enough "likes."

Like video games, social media has a potentially harmful dark side that can take a huge toll on women's confidence. The volumes of damning data about the negative impact of social media are multiplying by the day. Five years ago, when I first started speaking on this issue, there were a few studies about this, but their messages were drowned out by the balancing view of all the *benefits* that social media provides, such as speeding up communication, providing support, and connecting like-minded people engaged in important work around social causes, medical challenges, and education. Unquestionably, these are very real and important benefits. But they're just part of the story. The truth is, the more we study the impact of social media—especially on girls and women—the more potential damage we uncover.

For example, social media is a remarkably effective way to harass other people, especially women. A Pew Research Center report from 2017 found that 41% of Americans have been personally subjected to harassing behavior online, and 66% have witnessed these behaviors directed at others.[50] And 18% have been subjected to particularly severe forms of harassment online, such as physical threats, harassment over a sustained period, sexual harassment, or stalking. Among younger Americans, the situation is even worse: 67% of 18- to 29-year-olds have been the target of online harassment; for 41%, that harassment was severe. Among women—especially younger women—harassment is often sexual: 53% of women ages 18 to 29 say that someone has sent them explicit sexual images they did not ask for.

The effects of online harassment don't disappear when a woman hits "delete." They linger, interfering with her concentration, gnawing away at her confidence, and increasing her risk of anxiety and depression. And social media harassment doesn't just happen to women. It's also aimed at men, especially men who are not the straight white leaders in the male core power system. Anyone who is considered an "other" can expect to be targeted, especially if they're not white, gender-conforming, or straight. The human fear of being called out, embarrassed, or publicly shamed is quite universal, and employees bring the scars from these experiences with them to work.

Social media doesn't have to be harassing or threatening to chip away at confidence and interfere with women's mental health. A 2018 study by UK researchers found that spending more than an hour a day on social media is linked to poor body image, which in turn can lead to eating disorders, depression, and feelings of isolation.[51] And because females tend to use social media more than males, they experience a greater negative impact—as social media use goes up, so too do social and emotional difficulties. A 2017 study published in the journal Clinical Psychological Science found that adolescents who spend more time on new media such as social media and smartphones were more likely to report mental health issues than those who spent more time on non-screen activities such as sports, in-person interaction, and homework. This "may account for increases in depression and suicide," the researchers concluded.[52]

Desire to be Liked

With its emphasis on getting "likes" social media platforms reinforce perfectionism and lead users to compare themselves with others on a non-stop basis. It's a no-win situation: When we look at someone else's postings about themselves, their significant others, their vacations, their children, and their jobs, we see carefully curated views that don't represent their everyday reality. But we take them at face value, compare them to our own lives, and judge ourselves as lacking. We compare the best in others to the worst in ourselves, and never come out ahead. These assessments not only result in resentment and disappointment, but they take power away from ourselves and hand it off to others.

We know that the average person spends nearly two hours a day on social media—more time than we spend eating and drinking, non-digital socializing, and grooming.[53] And we know that girls and women engage in this confidence-sapping pastime more than men. While the boys are playing video games that build them up as powerful men, the girls are on social media, catching up with friends and having fun, and also having their confidence chipped away, receiving one message after another that says they're not good enough.

Violent video games and social media both come to the same conclusion—that the viewpoint that really matters is the one that sees the world through male eyes, with females playing supporting roles as objects of pleasure for men. Both the boys and the girls internalize this message, which follows them all the way from adolescence to your office.

The most stunning thing about sexually violent video games and confidence-robbing social media platforms is that they so baldly reinforce the dominant male/subjugated female world view. With very few exceptions, they've been created by men, they are controlled by men, and their profits go to men. (Even now, years into the Internet age, women are underrepresented in high tech; a 2018 analysis of 6,000 companies by the software platform Carta found that overall, men own 91% of employee and founder equity in Silicon Valley, leaving women a scant 9%.[54])

Someday we'll probably look back at these early days of video gaming and social media and wonder how in the world we allowed them and the companies that created them to launch and grow with no regulation of the content they carry, the privacy they invade and sell, or the acute and chronic harm they do to the people who use them. Let's hope that changes soon.

Coming Up Next

So far, we've looked at the origin of the male hegemonic power myth and its pervasiveness within the major forms of entertainment and communication consumed by our society. We've seen how it shapes the warped view of gender that not all but some of your male and female employees carry with them, and we've examined how it makes girls and women feel less safe and less valued. This belief system brands itself on children from a young age and is reinforced by countless factors in our culture. It's no wonder that gender bias is so deeply grounded in every part of American society, including our workplaces. Before we start looking at ways in which business leaders can bring about meaningful change by operating with a Dignity Mindset, we have one more crucial area to explore: How the male power belief system expresses itself in colleges and universities, and how those forces affect the men and women you hire and employ. College is the final step in the birth-to-workplace continuum that reinforces the male power belief system in which men dominate and women are subordinate, where men are up and women are down. Understanding that final stop before employment will ensure a comprehensive awareness of where the gender bias in your organization formed, how it was reinforced, and why it has such a strong influence.

CHAPTER 5

Gender Bias on Campus

"Think what it means to be a man who cares about women: It means you don't want to see any of them treated like dirt. You don't want to see any of them living in fear of violence."

— Michael Kaufman, author of *Man Talk: What Every Guy Oughta/Gotta Know About Good Relationships*

Celery. That's what Michael Kaufman, a researcher, author, and co-founder of the White Ribbon Campaign, the largest international effort of men working to end violence against women, uses to describe the way people learn gender stereotypes. Stick a piece of celery in a cup of water dyed with purple food coloring, and a day or two later the celery will be purple, because it will have absorbed the water in the cup. Kaufman says our brains are the same way. As they grow, they are heavily influenced by the social and natural environments that surround us.

"And since this is happening in a male-dominated society where gender really matters, this is a process where we internalize gender expectations, ideals, relations— gender power—right into our brains," Kaufman writes. "We don't simply learn to fit a stereotype; our brains become *gendered*."[55] In other words, we soak up the belief systems around us like celery absorbs colored water.

This soaking up of male/female gender expectations goes on throughout childhood and into young adulthood. It creates a gender bias that is wired into so many girls as well as boys in ways that are both overt and invisible.

In previous chapters, we traced the path of gender bias that individuals in our culture travel while making their way from childhood to the workplace. From their earliest days, your future employees absorb the impact of male power belief systems that legitimize the subordination of girls and women. This belief system is reinforced in primary school, secondary school, entertainment, video games, and social media. Unfortunately, bias reinforcement continues in college.

It would be nice to believe that when young people arrive at college, the spirit of academic openness would allow a less gender-biased, more constructive belief system to replace the male hegemonic power myth. In other words, that college would drain the purple water of bias out of their brains. But that's not what typically happens. Instead, college tops off a lifetime of immersion in gender-biased belief systems with a potentially toxic mix of peer pressure, excessive alcohol use, and, at some schools, campus traditions that glorify male misbehavior. This routinely manifests as overt and hidden gender bias, and in the worst cases, as sexual assault and rape.

Sexual violence on college campuses isn't just a problem for colleges, however. What is often described as the "rape culture" on college campuses also impacts the businesses in which college graduates work after leaving the ivy halls. The lessons both genders learn in college can be varied, but when gender bias is central to the experience, these lessons represent a roadblock that can stand between businesses, gender equity, and organizational success.

Having a clear awareness of this societal problem and how college culture affects men and women in the workplace can allow you to understand and counteract its impact within your organization.

Campus Life: The Stop Just Before the Job Search

On campus, the male power belief system has contributed to the flourishing of what many experts call the "rape culture." Kaufman describes rape culture as an environment in which "we trivialize and even excuse sexual violence. When this violence becomes the subject of jokes and everyday speech ("I raped that exam"), we trivialize sexual assault. In a rape culture, violence is portrayed as powerful and sexy. Violent degrading sex gets celebrated, like in a lot of porn. This also means that our judicial system still doesn't take the crime seriously enough."[56]

When college students become job applicants, this mentality is not magically corrected, and it's one of the reasons so many organizations face sexual harassment lawsuits.

You've certainly heard some of the horror stories about sexual assault and rape on college campuses. A girl goes to a party or bar, a guy or several guys slip something into her drink to incapacitate her, and then they assault or rape her. Or a guy invites a girl back to his room after a night of partying and decides that even though she says no, she must mean yes. Or because she is too drunk to offer any kind of consent, he goes ahead and has sex with her anyway. Or a guy forces himself on a girl in an empty classroom or dorm hallway. Or a guy gets angry because his girlfriend flirted with another guy, so he forces her to have sex with him. Or a guy walks by the basement laundry room one evening and sees a lone woman folding her clothes and sexually assaults her; afterward, he goes on with his night, but she withdraws from school.

Whether in college or out in the world, rape, sexual assault, and harassment are demonstrations of power and dominance. When a man sexually assaults a woman, he controls her and dehumanizes her. He attempts to own her and oppress her, using her for his own edification with no regard for her agency. Remember, the male hegemonic power myth is a belief system that legitimizes the subordination of women because of the view that they simply aren't as valuable as men. Sexual assault is an unsurprising result of this world view.

To be sure, the vast majority of college men do not sexually assault women. "The problem is that the majority of us have remained silent about such abuse," Kaufman writes.

"Through our silence, we allow abusive words and behavior to continue."[57]

Aspects of rape culture don't just exist on college campuses: It's alive and well on sports teams and in some workplaces, too. In your office, it may manifest when men tease or shame male colleagues who hire, mentor, or engage with women as equal and worthy colleagues. As Simmons College President Helen Drinan, says, "Leadership is how you show up at the water cooler." What kind of leadership do the men on your team show at the water cooler? If one guy complains about gender inclusion in your organization, do other men speak up or just sip their water in silence? When a guy comments about the size of a female co-worker's breasts, do others tell him to stop being so unprofessional or just say nothing? Rape culture is about so much more than rape; it's about a world view that allows men to violate women with words as well as actions.

"We guys act tough, we act in control, we act like 'one of the boys,'" writes Kaufman. "Too often we keep quiet in the face of homophobia, racism, and other forms of bigotry.

Why? Because deep down we're scared of not being a 'real man.' This leads many of us to keep quiet when we see women around us getting hurt, getting humiliated, and getting talked about like sexual meat."[58]

And don't think the gender-biased culture on college campuses is limited to students; it manifests among faculty, too. In its 2017-2018 salary report, the American Academy of University Professors found that 93% of their participating institutions pay men more than women at the same rank.[59] And among full professors, men outnumber women by more than two to one, while a majority of assistant professors, instructors, and lecturers are women.[60] What message do you think this discrepancy sends the young men and women in college?

Bro Culture and the Straight White Man

"Bro culture" is another kind of misogynistic influence on college men. It encompasses a range of male-power behaviors, including excessive drinking, aggressive sports activities, fraternity hazing, playing violent/ sexually explicit video games, and verbally harassing women, gay men, people of color, and anyone who fails to qualify as a hyper-masculine bro. There's no room in bro culture for anyone who's not a bro, except as a sexual plaything or as a target for harassment or jokes.

Popular movies portray bro culture as harmless and fun. (Of course, they do; they're filmed from the viewpoint of the male gaze.) But it's not harmless to its victims. And it's not harmless when it becomes part of an organization's corporate culture, as it is in many companies that struggle with gender bias.

Bro culture is a driving force behind the sexism in Silicon Valley, according to Emily Chang, an executive producer at Bloomberg TV, a tech industry reporter, and author of the book *Brotopia: Breaking Up the Boys Club of Silicon Valley*. In a 2018 interview, Chang paints a picture of how one way that bro culture manifests in organizations, forcing impossible choices on women:

> "So much business in Silicon Valley gets done outside the office. We are talking about the party, the bar, the hotel lobby, the conference, maybe it's the hot tub. In a lot of situations, women are being put in uncomfortable positions where they're not able to be their best selves. I've spoken to so many women who said, I don't want to get into a hot tub and pitch investors my business while holding a beer. What woman wants to do that while wearing a bikini? A lot of the times it's their male managers that are inviting them out, and they're faced with this sort of catch-22, do I go and be part of the team? Of course, they're going to talk about work. Or do I stay and be that uncool kid and not get that opportunity?"[61]

When bro culture dominates in an organization, the struggle to hire and retain women, people of color, and anyone who's not a straight white bro is enormous, expensive, and, as lawsuits against companies such as Nike, Uber, and Google[62] demonstrate, potentially damaging to a company's brand. This is true even when the organization's board of directors is attempting to show leadership on diversity. One wonders, in the era of #MeToo, how leaders in companies steeped in bro culture don't see the force of change in front of them, though the perspective of the male gaze suggests the reason for their myopia.

By replacing bro culture with a culture that aligns with a Dignity Mindset, which is built on the belief that everyone in the organization has the same worth and the same fundamental human needs as everyone else, leaders can position their companies to start achieving the success that organizations with diverse workforces enjoy. It's unlikely, though, that you're going to get much support for that from the dominant power group: the bros themselves.

What Tomorrow's Leaders Learn in College

The rape culture and bro culture in colleges teach young men that they have permission to treat women as they please, just a year or two before they enter the job market. Here's just one example of this dynamic: In 2016, the Harvard men's soccer team had its season suspended after it was revealed that the team had created a document "that, in sexually explicit terms, individually assessed and evaluated freshmen recruits from the … women's soccer team based on their perceived physical attractiveness and sexual appeal," according to the school's newspaper, the *Harvard Crimson*. The "scouting report," that evaluated each female recruit also assigned a highly graphic hypothetical sexual position in addition to her position on the soccer field.[63]

While considering this, please think about the women who, having done nothing wrong except existing, woke up for class one morning, freshman year, and suddenly found themselves shamed, humiliated, and very publicly called out at school. Imagine a 17- or 18-year-old young woman, guilty of nothing, just trying to get good grades and show what she can do on a soccer field. Think of your own child, innocently beginning another day and having to face this shop of horrors, unprepared, unarmed, and utterly unprotected, including by the university to which you entrusted her and to whom you pay tuition. Think! And by now, you know enough to begin connecting the dots yourself: how an experience like this can feed the imposter syndrome that women show up with at work.

Here's another example, from Stanford: A couple of years ago, emails from Snapchat founder Evan Spiegel's college days at Stanford University were published online. "In the emails—most of which we can't quote from due to sexually graphic content and obscene language—Spiegel wrote about making 300 Jell-O shots to get sorority girls drunk, urinating on one conquest, and shopping for cocaine and marijuana," wrote the *Los Angeles Times*.[64] The article quotes Spiegel as saying he was "obviously mortified and embarrassed that my idiotic emails during my fraternity days were made public," adding that he was sorry and was a jerk to have written them. "They in no way reflect who I am today or my views towards women."

Are we to believe that Spiegel's belief system—which was learned and reinforced during a lifetime of exposure to toxic male-dominating cultural frameworks—experienced such an extraordinary turnaround in only a matter of a few years? Was he sorry for writing those emails, or sorry for getting caught having written them?

Eventually Spiegel founded Snapchat, an app whose original purpose was to enable users to send photographs that would magically disappear after being viewed. What kind of photos do you think Spiegel and his co-founders were creating their app for—daffodils in springtime? In March 2019, when the *Wall Street Journal*[65] published an article stating that Snap, Inc., the parent company of Snapchat, paid settlements to "at least three female employees who were let go in layoffs that they alleged disproportionately targeted women," it was not surprising. It's easy to imagine that a man who boasts about urinating on women and getting sorority girls drunk for sex would create a corporate culture and, one could argue, a business that devalues and exploits women.

From College to Your Company

Sexual violence has obvious physical and emotional repercussions for college women immediately after they occur. These include higher rates of depression, anxiety, and posttraumatic stress disorder. These actions also leave long-lasting—in many cases, lifelong— scars on victims. A 2019 study published in *JAMA Internal Medicine* found that a history of sexual assault or sexual harassment is associated with significantly higher blood pressure, poorer sleep quality, and symptoms of depression and anxiety.[66]

Even women who are not sexually assaulted during college carry the burden of personal safety concerns all their lives. The fear of sexual assault stays with them, from the commute in the morning, to shuffling the kids to the bus, to parking in the work parking lot, and especially with that manager who often asks for a little hug at the end of a meeting. In Part II of this book we look at the fundamental human needs that can go unmet in biased situations. One of them is personal safety; when people don't feel safe, it's nearly impossible for them to realize their highest potential for self-actualization.

Men who harass and sexually assault women in the workplace count on women's fear. In work-related situations, women often experience what's referred to as sexual coercion. We heard many stories of this kind of behavior when the #MeToo movement gained traction. Sexual coercion is any unwanted sexual activity that happens after being pressured in non-physical ways. It occurs when a boss or manager uses his authority to pressure an employee into having sex, or when a co-worker threatens to spread rumors about a person unless they agree to have sex.

That we ask so much of women—to make it through the gauntlet from youth to work, and again sometimes at work—says so much about the strength of women, and their willingness to battle on even when it takes everything they have to do so. But it's important to remember that corralling all that strength takes energy that could be better spent on contributing their talents at work. When you have to focus on avoiding sexual harassment, it's difficult to put your best effort into a marketing report.

The collegiate experience gives very wide guardrails for male behavior. But it also creates fears in some of the many good men—men who get it and want to ally with women—who worry that women will misinterpret actions such as inviting them out for coffee after a meeting or having lunch after a sales call. One young man told me he made sure never to be alone in a room with a female colleague, because he worried that a comment or action would be misconstrued. His motivation makes sense, but unfortunately, his efforts to protect himself by avoiding women likely harms them more than him. Women don't want to be victimized, but they also don't want to be treated like plutonium.

So much benefit can come to our organizations and the people who work in them— both men and women—when we choose to vacate our own gender-biased echo chambers and engage in open conversations based on dignity, rather than belief systems that no longer serve us.

College, Confidence, and Imposter Syndrome

For women, exposure to the male power culture in college can reinforce feelings of self-doubt that arise during adolescence and are bolstered by exposure to social media and its unrealistic expectations. Social media tells girls that everyone else is prettier, happier, thinner, smarter, and more successful; college's rape/bro culture sends the message that their entire gender is "less than." As these ideas percolate through young women's minds they can tear away at self-confidence, leading to self-doubt and the development of imposter syndrome.

As we discussed in Chapter 4, imposter syndrome is the persistent feeling that an individual's success has not been earned, deserved, or legitimately achieved as a result of their skills and efforts. People with imposter syndrome experience chronic self-doubt about their abilities despite ample evidence to the contrary. It is driven by a fear of failure; if you suffer from imposter syndrome and you experience failure, it offers proof that you don't deserve to be where you are and that you are indeed a fake.

Imposter syndrome causes women to be afraid to speak up, ask questions, or take chances because of the fear that any weakness or mistake will be interpreted as failure or will expose them as a fraud. Of course, the irony is that when people don't put themselves out there because of a fear of being exposed or publicly failing, these behaviors can have a negative impact on their performance and growth.

Imposter syndrome grows from seeds planted throughout childhood and adolescence that tell women they're not good enough. These messages may come from parents, teachers, or churches, but even when girls are lucky enough to escape bias from those sources, the steady drumbeat of subjugation that comes from the male power myth can build feelings that lead to imposter syndrome. When girls watch movies framed through the male gaze, when they hear debasing trash talk from boys on the school bus, when they hear music that celebrates men who use women, when they see the way women are treated in video games, when they learn about things like the gender pay gap, when they see men at the highest levels in our country being allowed to get away with sexual harassment, when they see example after example after example of women being subordinated to men—that's the steady drumbeat of female inferiority that pounds imposter syndrome into them. Then college cements it all. It's hard to keep believing you are good enough when you receive so many messages from the culture that you're not. What's astonishing is not how many women suffer from imposter syndrome/lack of confidence, but the fact that any women at all manage to escape it.

Breaking down gender-biased belief systems and replacing them with a Dignity Mindset within your organization can create an atmosphere that fosters confidence. An important first step is recognizing that in many organizations women truly are treated as imposters because, quite simply, they are not men. (If you're a man, imagine how you would feel if you attended a baby shower with twenty women. You'd likely feel quite out of place.) In environments aligned with a Dignity Mindset, many of the constructs that reinforce imposter syndrome are torn away, allowing women to feel that they are welcomed, and their intelligence and hard work are respected.

Unlearning the Lessons of Bias: Belief Systems and Change

A belief system is a set of beliefs, principles, or ideologies that guide an individual or a group. We all experience the influence of various belief systems and worldviews. Religions are belief systems. Capitalism is a belief system. Environmentalism is a belief system. Feminism is a belief system. Belief systems can be shared by millions, or they can be individual—we all hold our own personal belief systems.

Belief systems are powerful things. As we've discussed, the male power belief system is one of the most prevailing belief systems, having influenced human life for over 8,000 years. But don't confuse power with unchangeability. Belief systems can be changed, and in fact they're a central part of how leaders grow and develop. I often coach very smart people who were trained, for example, to be the smartest person in the room. That belief system, and its negative effects on teams, is something we work to change so the team can be highly functional and productive. The same can be said of gender bias, and bias against those pushed to the margins because they don't look like straight white men in the C-suite.

Many organizations are already seeing the male power belief system shifting. We'll look at some examples of those companies in the second half of this book. We'll also look at how freeing it can be for men as well as women to shift a company's belief system from one that is built around male domination/female subordination to one that is aligned with a Dignity Mindset that recognizes the equal value of every human being.

It may seem like it would be comfortable to remain stuck in old belief systems, but the truth is, it's exhausting, including for the people digging in their heels. Refusing to evolve, remaining trapped in fear of zero-sum ideas (if she wins, I lose) is the real lose-lose proposition.

Kaufman already sees this starting to happen. "Across the country and around the world, we are now seeing a rapidly growing number of men who reject the narrow demands of manhood and who reject the notion of male superiority to women," he writes in his book, *The Time Has Come: Why Men Must Join the Gender Equality Revolution.*[67] "We see more men who are willing to be affectionate with their male friends. We see more men ... who show immense respect for female coworkers and colleagues. We see many men who are embracing a dramatic transformation in their role as fathers."

The male power belief system traps women, but it also traps men. Kaufman points out that no man can live up to all of the expectations that this belief system pushes onto them. Men "can't always be strong and fearless, have all the answers, be the economic provider, be ready and able to fight, be good with tools, good at sports, talking, and drinking, and fit seamlessly into the tight suit of manhood," Kaufman writes. "Not just a suit. A suit of armor. No man can pull it off."[68] When you lead your organization with a Dignity Mindset, you allow everyone to break out of the suit of armor that restricts their contributions. They still have to work hard and bring their A game to work every day, but without the heavy limitations imposed by dysfunctional belief systems, it's so much easier for them to excel.

As a leader, your job is to be an influencer and an agent of change. One of the most exciting parts about being a leader is that you have so many opportunities to learn new lessons, set new goals, and embrace new missions as the marketplace in which your organization competes changes. The best leaders embrace learning, growth, and change so they can always be ready to show leadership for the next mission. They anchor their organizations to a core set of values and a collective belief system that serves as a clear reference point for the choices and behaviors of everyone in their organization as they collaborate to achieve business success.

Coming Up Next

You now have a clear understanding of how gender bias impacts organizations and the way in which our culture nurtures it. You have a greater awareness of how male power belief systems, mainstream cinema, video games, social media, and certain types of college culture shape the world views of the individuals who work within your organization. Now it's time to look at the many ways in which you can start leading your company toward gender equity by shifting the underlying belief systems that fuel gender bias. In Part II of this book, we look at the specific steps you can take to start building and sustaining an equitable, dignity-based workplace where women and men feel valued and— most importantly, truly safe—to perform their very best work.

PART II

The Dignity Mindset Toolkit

Implementing a Dignity Mindset in Your Organization

"I believe we could paint a better world if we could learn to see it from all perspectives, as many perspectives as we possibly can. Because diversity is strength. Difference is a teacher. Fear difference, and you learn nothing."

— Hannah Gadsby, Australian comedian,
from her performance of "Nanette"

Imagine an organization where every employee has the same worth as every other employee. In this organization, every woman feels comfortable expressing herself and her individual talents authentically, without being forced to pretend she's a man. Every man feels comfortable expressing himself and his individual talents authentically, without feeling that he must follow out-of-date masculinity behavior scripts that fit his father's generation far better than his own.

Imagine an organization where people listen to, rather than talk over, each other; where contributions are appreciated for their value, rather than the gender or race of their source; where women have no fear of sexual harassment or assault; where men with skills and talents that are not traditionally "male" feel comfortable sharing them; where employees receive recognition from each other and from management for the outstanding quality of their contributions, rather than their ability to conform to a male-centric power culture; where people earn respect rather than demanding it.

Imagine an organization where all employees have the space to meet their own needs for safety, social belonging, self-esteem, and self-actualization while driving their company forward toward achieving its highest goals.

In an organization like this, teamwork thrives, creativity flourishes, empathy abounds, and confidence grows. Boundaries are removed to allow everyone's capabilities, knowledge, spirit, and experience to flow. Supportive, thoughtfully designed belief systems replace harmful, outdated ideologies. Employees learn how to communicate in ways that promote constructive conversation, trust, and positive change rather than blame; they feel comfortable giving and receiving feedback because they learn how to do so with support and respect. When brainstorming, employees feel confident taking risks because they trust their teammates to value and build upon their ideas.

An organization like this succeeds because its employees, freed from the burdens of gender stereotypes, bias, fear, and power play, can let down their guard and focus on performing at their highest possible level every day. Employees enjoy their jobs more, feel loyal to the organization, stay in their jobs longer, and work harder to support their organization's goals. They understand their organization's market and customers with greater clarity than their competitors. And when the organization succeeds, its employees feel an intrinsic sense of pride and look forward to continued achievements.

This organization may sound too good to be true, but it's not. This is what a dignity-based workplace looks like. And it's what your company can start to look like when you begin implementing the Dignity Mindset recommendations in this book.

What is Dignity?

If you embrace dignity, you believe that:

Everyone as the same worth and the same fundamental human needs as everyone else.

Having a Dignity Mindset means you look at every person, every interaction, and every decision through the lens of dignity. Other definitions of dignity focus only on worth, but I believe that full dignity must also address every person's fundamental human needs and the ways in which those needs go unmet in biased contexts.

Dignity and an organizational commitment to self-actualization come together to frame the **Dignity Mindset, which is based on the expectation that everyone in an organization should be safe and free to be their best and real self while pursuing excellence and business success.** A dignity-based organization flourishes under the leadership of individuals who have an abundance mentality and who are committed to ensuring that the primary focus of the organization stays on winning in its markets, not on consistent concerns about seizing political power from colleagues or achieving or maintaining power and dominance.

Fundamental Human Needs

What does it mean to create a workplace in which all employees have the opportunity to fulfill their fundamental needs while driving organizational success? Let's step back for a moment to a concept you may have learned about in college.

If you took Psych 101 as an undergrad, you probably studied a theory known as Maslow's Hierarchy of Needs. You may recall a pyramid that illustrates basic human needs. Toward the bottom of the pyramid are the most fundamental needs, and at the top are higher-level needs. Basically, the pyramid ranks human needs as Maslow defined them and illustrates his belief that needs must be met in a hierarchical way.

Physiological needs make up the base of Maslow's pyramid. These include necessities of everyday life, such as food, water, shelter, sleep, and sex. The next level addresses safety needs, which include personal and emotional security, as well as financial security and health. On the next levels are social belonging (friendship, family, and intimacy), followed by self-esteem (recognition and respect from others). Then, at the top of the pyramid is self-actualization, which is the realization of one's full potential. Our goal as humans is to self-actualize and achieve our full potential. In a dignity-based organization, this isn't just a personal goal, but a professional goal as well.

Maslow organized these needs in a pyramid to emphasize the idea that in order to meet higher-level needs, the most basic lower-level needs must first be achieved. For example, people are unlikely to be able to feel safe and secure (the second level) when they don't have a place to live or enough food to eat (the first level). Likewise, self-actualization (the top level) is far less likely when individuals lack social belonging (third level) or self-esteem (fourth level).

How does this relate to our discussion of dignity-based organizations and gender bias in the workplace? To understand the connection, let's look at that top level in Maslow's pyramid of needs: self-actualization. In order for people to self-actualize and realize their full potential, they must be meeting most or all of their fundamental needs on a fairly consistent basis. However, it is likely that many women (as well as men) who work in organizations that are *not* built around a commitment to dignity and gender equity are failing to have their most fundamental needs met on a daily basis.

In a workplace, self-actualization means that employees have the space, training, and management support to do their very best work. They can perform at their highest level, they receive recognition for doing excellent work, they feel free to take intellectual risks, and they feel comfortable and safe expressing their talents and ideas in an authentic way. That's what happens at the top of the pyramid in a workplace whose leaders adopt a Dignity Mindset.

But consider this: That type of self-actualization can't happen unless lower-level needs are being met. Women can't excel in a self-actualizing way when they're worried about feeling safe and secure (for example, safe from sexual harassment and unwanted advances and secure in the knowledge that their managers have their backs), if they feel they will be humiliated for taking intellectual risks (for example, during a brainstorming session), if they lack social belonging (for example, if they are left out of meetings or social events because they're not "one of the guys" or if their great ideas are appropriated by men), or if they are unlikely to receive recognition or respect from colleagues who minimize their contributions because of gender bias.

This applies to people of color and individuals in the LGBTQ community, too. How can they self-actualize at work and perform at their highest potential when they are unable to achieve the fundamental needs for safety, social belonging, and self-esteem? It is impossible.

Invisible Needs

In some cases, basic human needs can't be met because employees are encouraged not even to acknowledge them. This often occurs with men who have been so hemmed in by the male power barriers they grew up with and that permeate their organization that they can't even admit they have needs that don't fit into traditional male role expectations. Too many men find that their own personal manhood is defined not by their own needs, interests, and preferences, but by what our culture has decided they should and shouldn't need, want, and enjoy.

Under the rigid dictates of the male hegemonic power myth, even the straight white men who typically wear the suit of traditional manhood in our society, and who appear to have it all because their team has held power for 8,000 years, may not see their self-actualization needs met. Many of these men are so busy trying to uphold the image of the powerful man that society has forced onto them that they can't even think about what they *really* want out of life, let alone go after it. Sadly, they may not identify this missed opportunity until retirement, when they realize they've spent their career chasing goals forced on them by the male power myth, rather than walking a path that would have aligned with their own interests and values.

Psychologist Jack Sawyer explored this heartbreaking truth in his classic 1970 essay, "On Male Liberation." In it he wrote about how men who define themselves primarily by their performance as breadwinners risk missing out on fulfilling needs that lie beyond the narrow role of power holder in a hegemonic male system. In other words, their slavish adherence to traditional gender roles may prevent them from self-actualizing.

> "The process area of life—activities that are enjoyed for the immediate satisfaction they bring—are not part of the central definition of men's role. Yet the failure of men to be aware of this potential part of their lives leads them to be alienated from themselves and from others. Because men are not permitted to play freely, or show affect, they are prevented from really coming in touch with their own emotions. If men cannot play freely, neither can they freely cry, be gentle, nor show weakness— because these are

'feminine' not 'masculine.' But a fuller concept of humanity recognizes that all men and women are potentially both strong and weak, both active and passive, and that these and other human characteristics are not the province of one sex."[69]

The last thought in that quote—that a fuller concept of humanity defines various traits and characteristics as being human, rather than male or female—is a core value in a dignity-based organization. People perform best when they are free to be themselves and to own the traits and characteristics that are true to their own personalities, rather than to gender expectations.

In a dignity-based workplace, leaders take steps like the ones described in the following pages to clear away the debris of gender expectations and bias that stands between their employees and exceptional, self-actualized performance at work. When employees are meeting their higher-order needs at work, their whole self is in alignment in a healthy, fulfilled way. They:

- Are not hiding themselves, guarding themselves, or trying to show up at work every day as someone else.
- Can take off the coat of armor that they previously had to wear in order to survive each day.
- Can stop wasting their time trying to fit into gender roles or belief systems that are not native or true to them.
- Can go to work expecting to flourish, not just survive.
- Have the space to show up at work as their true, authentic selves and use their talents and gifts within a framework of openness and strength.

When those things happen, their leaders can just stand back and watch them shine.

This applies to men as well as women. Men who have the freedom to break out of traditional male power gender expectations (in part by stepping away from the gender bias they grew up with) can choose to take on non-traditional male gender roles in workplaces. They don't have to talk down to women in order to win the approval of other men. They don't have to hijack women's ideas and present them as their own. They don't have to laugh at sexist jokes and pretend they don't have emotions. They can stand up for women who are marginalized or underappreciated. They can take advantage of paternity leave or go home early for a child's sporting event or parent-teacher conference without feeling that the other men are making fun of them. They can act in accordance with their own values. And when they have the space to be true to themselves, they can thrive, which leads to self-actualization and organizational success.

By creating workplaces based on Dignity Mindset principles, both women and men discover the freedom to self-actualize in ways that are best for them as individuals, not as members of their gender. The Dignity Mindset makes space for *everyone* in the organization to self-actualize. People who feel happier work better. Rather than checking out jobs at other companies, they can focus all their energy on contributing to their company's success. How wonderful it is when humans have the freedom to be their authentic selves—their best, most productive selves—rather than living out roles forced on them by others.

Rebalancing Zero-Sum Belief Systems

Many of today's organizations operate under a zero-sum paradigm, which means every exchange is approached with a winner/loser framework. In order for one person to win, another must lose. In an organization, this approach can lead people to believe that if their group (gender, race, sexual orientation) shares power, it will forfeit various advantages in order for those advantages can be given to other groups. Zero-sum thinking is harmful for organizations and workers because it is built on a foundation of scarcity rather than growth. It creates limits and leads to competitiveness rather than cooperation.

A dignity-based organization is definitely not zero-sum. It is not driven by a power mentality that creates winners and losers *inside* the organization. Rather, it's a situation in which the shared, underlying belief system is about achieving breakthrough performance for everyone—and the organization—by being generous with and supportive of each other. As the saying goes, a candle loses nothing by lighting another candle. That's how it is in a dignity-based workplace. Instead of *excluding*, circles of people are opened *to include* different viewpoints, styles, strengths, and skills.

Within dignity-based organizations, the paradigm of outsiders needing to mask or change who they are to fit in with the straight white male core power structure is turned around: Those with power build *their* skills to ensure they're "other-fluent."

When you start to reverse zero-sum thinking in your organization, people can be themselves rather than trying to fit into rigid roles. Women don't have to pretend to be men in order to succeed, men don't have to pretend to embrace traditional male roles that don't fit them, and people of color don't have to "act white" to get ahead. There's no need for color-blindness or gender-blindness. Viewpoints such as, "I don't see gender," or "I don't see skin color," for example, are replaced with "I see you as you are and I want to work to understand *you*, and *your* experience, as part of sharing power and making sure you feel true membership in this organization." Like the finest coaches, leaders whose values align with a Dignity Mindset create the optimal environment for all to participate, and they model the inclusion of everyone's voices. It allows them to *be* who they are rather than trying to *change* who they are.

7 Dignity Mindset Tools

Creating a dignity-based organization is about replacing the old male hegemonic belief system with a belief system based on dignity: Every person has the same worth, and the same fundamental human needs, as every other person. You can do that by removing barriers and giving your people the space, training, support, and freedom to be their best. That's the big idea. In the sections that follow, we'll talk specifics: the things you can do to move your organization from a zero-sum culture to one with a shared belief system about inclusion, equal worth, and generosity that honors the people who are your talent and drives distinctive business success.

In Part II of this book, we look at seven of the most helpful tools in a system designed to change the belief systems and behaviors that contribute to gender bias in your organization. Each of these Dignity Mindset tools includes a variety of strategies and tactics that can be integrated into your organization; you can use them to adopt a Dignity Mindset for yourself and transform your company into a dignity-based organization. These tools can become part of the core operating processes in your business; they include a wealth of strategies and tactics that can facilitate optimal contribution and performance while creating the space for everyone in your organization to meet their fundamental needs.

Dignity-based organizations are, in their essence, oriented toward learning. Learning organizations thrive and remain relevant because they emphasize constant skill-building and growth, rather than the mastery and repetition of the same old skills. People who are in learning orientation mode day in and day out become comfortable with vulnerability and openness, because those traits lead to the best kind of learning. Playing it safe leads only to selective learning; making a safe space for vulnerability enables the most wonderful kind of growth and development.

If you're thinking that allowing yourself to become vulnerable to make way for growth and change sounds difficult, you're right! It is! If you feel a bit on edge as you step up to make this transition, congratulations—that means you're on the right track.

Be a Dignity-Driven Leader

"This world is changing enormously. In any position in a company
you need to work very hard on learning new skills every day, but
you also need to unlearn some of the old skills from the past."

— Paul Polman, former CEO, Unilever

In a dignity-based business, both the organization and the people who work within it have the space to thrive and succeed. When bias give way to belief systems built around a commitment to dignity, trust increases and creativity flourishes. Employees feel more willing to let down their guard and focus on collaborating and performing at their highest possible levels. Working in a company in which leadership has committed to a Dignity Mindset frees people to reach their maximum potential.

As a leader, you play a crucial role in establishing, defining, communicating, and modeling a Dignity Mindset within your organization. That begins by making sure you truly understand what dignity is. It bears repeating: **Dignity is the belief that everyone in an organization has the same worth and the same fundamental human needs as everyone else.** Having a Dignity Mindset means you look at each interaction, decision, and hire through the lens of dignity, keeping in mind that everyone you come in contact with has the same worth and the same fundamental human needs as everyone else, no matter what their gender or background.

When I ask CEOs to define dignity, they often can't. They may have some feelings about what it means—for example, they may think that dignity is similar to respect, or that it is simply the act of listening to people. But it's important to point out that respect and dignity are not the same thing. Dignity is a given; we all have it and deserve it. But respect is something we earn through our actions, behaviors, and choices. When a group of people work together as a team in an organization, they all bring to the table an inherent worth and needs that they were born with as human beings—that's dignity. They have dignity no matter what their gender, sexual orientation, race, age, nationality, physical ability, cultural background, education, religion, choices, and so on. However, they *earn* respect for behaviors such as recognizing others' dignity, working hard, performing at the highest possible level, making choices that show integrity, apologizing for mistakes, and showing consideration to others.

Understanding the difference between dignity and respect is important in any discussion about gender bias and diversity. Diversity and inclusion initiatives fail when they demand universal respect for everyone, no matter what their contribution. That's just discouraging. Workers must earn the respect of their colleagues and leaders by delivering the kind of outstanding performance that drives organizational success.

Start with Yourself

As a leader, you take on the responsibility of recasting the pre-existing cultural systems in your organization in a new light—a dignity-based light. You do this by inspiring and educating the people in your organization and modeling Dignity Mindset behavior. But before you can successfully lead others, you must identify and change your own biases. You can't lead with dignity unless you embrace it as one of your own authentic truths. Once you do, you'll find it easier than you might expect to create a culture of gender equality and cultural diversity in your organization.

Opening your eyes to your own biases can be hard work for anyone, but the learning curve can be especially steep for straight white men who have grown up with top billing in the male power system and who have little or no experience being on the receiving end of bias. So, it's hard to identify your own biases, but it's certainly not impossible. As a successful leader you've done many difficult things—you're no stranger to hard work. Assuming you are serious about seeing and changing your biases, there's no reason you can't accomplish this important piece of personal development work.

The first step in this process is to take an honest look at yourself and your actions, both in the present and the past. As you read the chapters in the first part of this book, where we discussed hegemonic masculinity, the male gaze in movies, the diminishing of women in video gaming, the bro culture in college campuses and beyond, and other bias contexts in our society, what parts of it rang true for you? What shocked you? What made you feel uncomfortable? What parts of those narratives reflected your personal story and perspective? As you work on uncovering your own biases, consider going back to those chapters and rereading them with those questions in mind.

And by the way, if you believe you don't have any hidden biases, that's the very first opinion you should challenge. *Everyone* has hidden biases.

As you seek to root out your biases, use a spirit of empathy to take yourself out of your own personal frame of reference (gender, race, sexual orientation, and so on) and imagine yourself as the "other" who must confront biases built around their "otherhood" every day. Think deeply about how it would feel to be left out of meetings, paid less, spoken over, ignored, harassed, or marginalized in any way because of otherhood.

Don't just *think* about otherhood—really try it on and see how it feels. (Do this in your mind for now, but later we'll look at artificial intelligence tools that can make this experience feel even more real.) Carry your empathetic otherhood with you as you go through your day, attend meetings, and interact with people. How would your experiences change if you were "other than" what you are? What biases do you recognize, either in yourself or others? Do you feel yourself getting angry as you notice biased behavior occurring before your eyes? Explore these feelings—what do they tell you about yourself and your assumptions?

Question Your Biases

Biased thoughts tend to be automatic and unexplored. They are such a part of who we are and what we believe that we tend to take them as gospel truth without ever really subjecting them to questioning and choice.

Because gender bias tends to be poured into us beginning at birth, as we discussed in Part I of this book, it is typically as invisible to us as the air we breathe. However, a process of observation and questioning can uncover bias.

Notice the automatic thoughts, assumptions, and opinions that enter your mind when you spend time with people who are other than you in terms of gender, race, sexual orientation, and so on. As you start to increase your awareness of these automatic thoughts and opinions, ask yourself some of the following questions about them:

- Is this opinion accurate and realistic?
- Is it based on fact or assumptions?
- What evidence is there to support it?
- Is it possible that I have misinterpreted the evidence that I believe supports this opinion?
- Am I basing my opinion on feelings rather than facts?
- Where did I learn this opinion?
- What might the person I'm considering say about my opinion?

Once you subject your automatic thoughts and opinions to careful questioning, you can pass judgment on them and decide whether they represent the Dignity Mindset approach. If they do, hold on to them. If not, work to reframe them in a way that better reflects your commitment to dignity. Your thoughts guide your actions, so taking the time to examine and restructure any biased thinking pays off when you set out to take dignity-based leadership action.

You can also learn more about your own biases by taking an Implicit Association Test (IAT), a tool created by Project Implicit to measure attitudes and stereotypes. Project Implicit is a nonprofit organization launched by an international collaboration of researchers. The test can be found at: https://implicit.harvard.edu/implicit/takeatest.html.

Leaders who put themselves through these paces often tell me that once they start to see bias in themselves and others, they can't un-see it. They feel shocked and embarrassed that they haven't recognized it before. If you feel this way, congratulations—you're beginning to open your mind to dignity.

Let Dignity-Based Values Drive Decisions

Dignity-focused leaders make a conscious commitment to belief that everyone in their organization, from people at the first rung of the corporate ladder to the highest-level executives, has the same worth and the same fundamental human needs as everyone else. They commit to full gender equality, not only because it's a smart business strategy but because it's the right thing to do. In other words, they don't just proclaim dignity and equality as goals—they internalize these values themselves and allow them to guide their actions.

With dignity and every other core value, it comes down to this: If you don't believe it, the people you lead won't believe it, either. Values require authenticity. Unless they live within you, the tactics and expenses you incur to change behaviors of the workforce will not happen, or they may happen briefly before returning to prior stasis.

Leaders who truly embody the Dignity Mindset hold dignity and gender equity as essential values and core beliefs. It's important for leaders to spend time defining and committing to their core beliefs because doing so makes decisions so much easier. Having solid core beliefs in place guides you as make decisions and choices. The most successful people I have met in business are those who have invested serious effort in the process of consciously examining and refreshing their belief systems. They're able to do what's right and to have the guts to make potentially unpopular decisions because they're following values that they hold within them rather than responding to an ever-changing set of outside forces.

An amazing example of decision-making based on core beliefs comes from Marc Benioff, chairman and co-CEO at Salesforce, a cloud-based customer relationship management platform.[70] [71] Salesforce has made a major commitment to equality and dignity and includes this pledge in its mission statements: "At Salesforce, equality is a core value, and we're taking action to advance equality across four key areas: equal pay, equal opportunity, equal education, and equal rights."

Having that core value in place drove Benioff's actions in a very important way. During a 2018 interview with Lesley Stahl at *60 Minutes*, Benioff explained that when his chief personnel officer, Cindy Robbins, told him in 2015 that she felt Salesforce had a gender pay gap problem, he didn't believe her.[72] "That's not possible here," he recalls saying. The company had made hiring, promoting, and retaining women a top priority, so Benioff felt there was no way the company could have a pay gap.

"I suspected there was some level of disparity because [as of 2015 we had] never really had this as part of our pay philosophy or as our pay culture," Robbins said during the same interview. Benioff agreed to do a pay assessment just to prove Robbins wrong. "And what I told Marc was, 'The one thing we can't do is, do the assessment, look under the hood, see a big dollar sign, and shut the hood.'" Benioff agreed that if a pay gap was found, the company would spend whatever was necessary to close it.

To Benioff's shock, the audit showed that the company did indeed pay women less than men. The pay gap existed "through the whole company, every division, every department, every geography," Benioff said. To remedy the situation, Benioff dedicated an initial $3 million to correct the discrepancy, and more than 10% of the women at Salesforce saw their paychecks increase.

Benioff said he felt happy with the outcome. But then, a second audit showed that Salesforce still had a pay gap. "It turned out we had bought about two dozen companies. And guess what? When you buy a company, you just don't buy its technology, you don't buy its culture, you also buy its pay practices," Benioff says. The company then invested an additional $3 million in 2017 to further adjust compensation gaps for gender, race, and ethnicity.[73] Further audits showed a need for additional adjustments. As of this writing, Salesforce says it has spent a total of $10.3 million to ensure equal pay for equal work within the organization.[74] Closing pay gaps is clearly *not* a one-and-done situation.

Consider the Benefits

As Benioff discovered, leading with dignity and correcting problems caused by gender bias can end up costing money. But think of how much a decision like that can save in terms of retaining great talent, showing potential hires that your organization confronts bias head-on, and giving employees the confidence that the company has their backs. Instead of wasting energy wondering if they're being taken seriously and receiving the same pay as men, the women at Salesforce can focus on doing their jobs to the best of their ability. Certainly Benioff would agree that those benefits are worth way more than the money the company spent to close its pay gap.

If Benioff hadn't made a true commitment to equality, both within the company and in his own mind, this story may have played out very differently. When Robbins challenged Benioff to order a pay audit, he may have chosen not to, either because of his assumption that a pay gap couldn't possibly exist in his company—which is what he believed—or because of concern that if a gap were uncovered, it would either have to be covered up or money would have to be spent to alleviate it. But because of Benioff's clear commitment to equality, he allowed his decision-making on the audit and the salary adjustments to be guided by his values. (The company also stands out for offering on-site childcare, generous family leave, and flexible schedules.)

Fully embracing a commitment to the values of dignity and gender equity gives leaders confidence to make decisions that could ruffle feathers within their organization. Operating from this solid base allows leaders to confront bias from a position of strength. Rather than walking on eggshells, as many leaders find themselves doing in the #MeToo era, they can move forward with self-assurance by deeply educating themselves about issues related to gender bias. From this education comes a fluency that they can bring to discussions with stakeholders within their organization. It also leads to personal growth, as leaders reinforce their ability to model unbiased thinking and behavior while confronting environmental and internalized bias within their organization.

One of the top fears that leaders (and all employees) have is to appear incompetent or unprepared in front of colleagues. However, through self-exploration, commitment to values, and continued self-education, individuals at all levels can act with greater confidence.

Free Yourself to Learn from Others

Leaders can expedite their gender equity discovery process by reaching out to others who have the capacity to teach. Significant learning can come from diversity professionals, other leaders who have already made a Dignity

Mindset journey, and executive coaches who specialize in gender inclusion and diversity. Wise, experienced teachers, coaches, and mentors can serve as true and honest brokers who guide you on through the process of developing your Dignity Mindset and taking steps to lead your organization in a way that allows it to function with cultural coherence.

If you're lucky, your organization's executive director of diversity and inclusion can serve as a trusted resource. In the best-case scenario, your D&I Department is led by someone with a Dignity Mindset who is not only skilled at creating policies and programs that encourage diversity, but who understands how to create a workplace that makes room for all workers to contribute their unique perspectives and talents. This may not be an option if your organization's CDO and D&I Department were staffed to fit into the culture of a biased or unenlightened executive team, however. Another possible resource is your chief human resources officer, assuming that person operates with the values and belief systems of a Dignity Mindset.

You may also turn to a highly trained executive coach who specializes in gender and inclusion. Executive coaches work one-on-one with leaders to assess strengths and challenges, identify values, set goals, build skills, take actions, and establish accountability through a process that leads to personal and organizational success.

Of course, asking for guidance and reaching out to other leaders for mentorship or advice can be challenging, especially for leaders who are more accustomed to giving assistance rather than requesting it. If the thought of reaching out for guidance makes you shudder, relax—that's a natural response. But it can also be a roadblock. You can overcome it by reminding yourself that success in all things is more likely when you can make a lifelong commitment to learning.

Leaders who commit to lifelong development understand that they are always going to continue acquiring new knowledge and skills. Unfortunately, too many leaders feel that the skills and knowledge that brought them to the highest levels of their organization are all they need to succeed; hubris prevents them from learning new things. Successful, innovative leaders not only recognize that development never ends, but that learning can come from many different sources.

Like many leaders, you may surround yourself with people who are just like you. But you can learn so much by talking with people who are "your other" in terms of gender, race, age, education level, and so on. Sitting down and engaging with people who are different from you—really talking, asking questions, and listening to their answers—can provide you with exceptional learning opportunities.

Learning requires a willingness to be vulnerable. Many but not all executives hate the idea of vulnerability, because they equate it with weakness. But it's not. Being vulnerable means being authentic and open, and with authenticity and openness, the best kinds of development and growth can occur. "Vulnerability is not weakness," says Brené Brown, a research professor at the University of Houston and author of *Daring Greatly: How the Courage to Be Vulnerable Transforms the Way We Live, Love, Parent, and Lead.* "Vulnerability is the birthplace of love, belonging, joy, courage, empathy, and creativity. It is the source of hope, empathy, accountability, and authenticity. If we want greater clarity in our purpose or deeper and more meaningful spiritual lives, vulnerability is the path."

Brown's view that "you have to walk through vulnerability to get to courage" makes so much sense in terms of embracing the Dignity Mindset, because it can be such a challenge to accept vulnerability. However, when you do, you soon begin to learn things about yourself and others that you never even *knew* you didn't know. Allowing yourself to be vulnerable also makes it easier to empathize with the otherhood of people who are targeted by bias.

Start Taking Action Now

As you work on changing your mindset, defining your own biases, growing, and developing new dignity-based leadership skills, you can start taking steps to reduce gender bias in your organization right away. There's no need for you to wait until you reach an arbitrary level of mastery to begin bringing about change—you can hit the ground running today. Even the smallest actions can have a snowball effect as people who behave with bias recognize your dignity leadership and people who are harmed by bias feel your support.

Leading the way to workplace gender equity can begin in small ways like the ones that follow.

Question What You See

When you look around in a meeting and notice there are few or no women at the table, ask why. During the uncomfortable silence that follows, ask for input about which women *should* be present. Show leadership by waiting for responses—it sends the message that this is everyone's problem, not just yours. Consider rescheduling the meeting for a time when more women can attend and designate the people who will be responsible for inviting them.

At Salesforce, when Benioff noticed there were no women in the room for many leadership meetings, he took action, deciding that he wouldn't have any more meetings that weren't at least one-third women. "This is part of who I have become as a leader," Benioff has said. "You can't be a great CEO and say that I'm not committed to gender equality today. I don't think it's possible."

Make Space for Women's Voices

In meetings, ask the women in the room for their point of view. In doing so you not only show them and the men in the room that women's voices matter to you, but you also signal to the women that you take them seriously; they are in the room to contribute, not just to even up the male/female numbers.

Call Out Biased Behavior

Create a meeting culture that has zero tolerance for behaviors such as interrupting, excessive monologuing, and mansplaining ("Let me help you understand what Janet is trying to say.") If you're not particularly strong at running meetings, work with your HR people or a corporate coach to improve your skills.

Keep Your Eyes Open

Notice how employees split up at lunch or in the executive dining room. If tables look like a junior high lunchroom, it's time to tell the men to start including women at their tables. Lots of business gets discussed during these downtimes, and if women aren't at the table, they miss out.

Reconsider Socializing Routines

If after-work get-togethers are a big part of your corporate culture, consider a shift. Drinks after work, weekend golfing outings, and similar activities can be quite exclusionary, not just of women but of various "others" such as older employees, people who make family a priority, and so on. Remember, dignity is the belief that *everyone* in an organization has the same worth and the same fundamental human needs as everyone else. One of those fundamental needs is social belonging, but that need can't be met at work when some people know that everyone is getting together without them.

Unbeknownst to you, making changes to socializing habits in your organization may help employees whose otherhood goes beyond gender or race, such as the recovering alcoholics who are put in the position of dealing with that issue at drinking events, the single parents who would rather be home with the kids, and the introverts who conduct business far more effectively in a meeting room than a cocktail lounge, but who attend social events because they feel their careers could be damaged if they don't. Leaders can reshape the social aspect of the culture of their teams by removing these forced-choice dilemmas. And remember, it's not enough just to say, "Well, if Suzanne doesn't want to be left out of our social events, let's go ahead and invite her for bourbon and cigars in Bob's hot tub!" Inclusion is more nuanced than that; leaders need to be more sophisticated than that.

Ask yourself this: In what other ways can you convene that ensure that all colleagues can participate? Rather than going out for drinks after work, perhaps you can hold a social hour on Friday afternoon at 4 p.m., for example. And instead of an off-site golf tournament that leaves non-golfers out, choose an activity with a lower likelihood of gender-based mastery, such as archery. Point out to others how exclusionary after-hours activities look and feel to those who are not present; hold others accountable when they plan or attend such activities and ask them if they realize that leaving some team members out can undercut confidence and increase resentment. And if you do participate in a social activity at which some colleagues with a stake in the conversations aren't present, reach out to them afterwards and fill them in on what they missed.

Men on your team may express annoyance when you start making changes to the social culture in your company. Why should they have to give up dinners, drinks, weekend parties, and golf? Because it's not about them. It's about you making choices that are best for everyone in the organization and for the organization itself. Leaders must take unpopular stands all the time. And although the men who complain won't admit it, you're actually doing them a favor, because gender-balancing changes like these are not a fad. They're the way of the future. Men who are angry about things like changing after-hour social norms must learn that a very important part of avoiding career obsolescence is learning about the negative impact of some of the old ways of doing business. Bringing these guys into the 21st Century workplace may be painful for them, but the truth is, you're doing them a favor. This is what the future looks like.

Create an Inclusion Institute

*"Even folks with the best intentions can sometimes
get swept along by their biases."*[75]

— Emily V. Troiano, vice president of the Catalyst Information Center

Organizations that prosper invest in rigorous learning and development (L&D) departments. L&D's mandate is to identify knowledge gaps, create effective learning opportunities to fill those gaps, and ensure that employees continue to develop throughout their careers. Providing your employees with the best L&D helps your organization grow and succeed. When every individual in a company is in a constant state of learning, they thrive and remain relevant—and so does their employer.

When leaders and organizations begin to operate under a Dignity Mindset, and as they make important shifts toward embracing diversity and inclusion, employees at all levels have much to learn. However, taking a traditional L&D approach may not offer the most effective or thorough game plan for changing belief systems that have elevated men over women for thousands of years. Modifying deeply ingrained beliefs about gender is far more complex than teaching the latest technology skills; a trainer can't just gather employees in the conference room, spend a few hours lecturing, and expect them to emerge transformed.

You'll recall from earlier chapters that the male hegemonic power myth is instilled in us from birth and is reinforced by movies, television, video games, social media, schooling, and various other cultural and social influences. Inspiring people to do the self-examination necessary to recognize their own biases and to change beliefs and behaviors requires a sophisticated, nuanced approach.

As a leader with a commitment to a Dignity Mindset, you can support the nuanced learning needed to drive change in biased employee belief systems by working with your L&D department to build an Inclusion Institute. So much more than just another L&D program, an Inclusion Institute takes an innovative, out-of-the-box approach that goes beyond standard L&D fare.

In this section, we'll examine what a successful Inclusion Institute is and what it can provide. At its best, an Inclusion Institute can be one of your most powerful tools in reversing bias and increasing gender equity in your organization.

What is an Inclusion Institute?

The concept of an Inclusion Institute goes much farther than the typical L&D program. Standard L&D works well for standard skills, but when it comes to diversity and inclusion, standard approaches often fall short. Shortsighted diversity training often gets pushed onto employees in response to a discrimination lawsuit against the company, a sexual harassment accusation against an executive, a critical news report, or some other precipitating event. These one-off training programs tend to be focused more on avoiding the next lawsuit than providing meaningful learning. Thoughtful, effective gender equity learning events are disappointingly rare. Most seem designed more to check boxes than to facilitate an evolution in thinking or changes in an organization's culture.

An in-house Inclusion Institute takes innovative, creative approaches to replacing biased belief systems with an empathetic Dignity Mindset. It facilitates changes of heart that move people from bias to a belief that everyone in the organization has the same worth and the same fundamental needs as everyone else. An Inclusion Institute embeds a commitment to dignity and diversity as a structural beam in the organizations, not just as boxes that need to be checked.

An Inclusion Institute is part brick and mortar—a real place within your facilities— and part virtual. It offers a wide range of resources, including experiences, classes, events, reading materials, workshops, and discussion groups. It provides support as well as training, meeting people where they are and providing them with the understanding and knowledge that helps them explore and challenge their own thinking about bias. Although accountability plays an important part in an Inclusion Institute's learning process, the most effective approaches are supportive and nonjudgmental rather than punitive. As we've discussed elsewhere in this book, most of the men who hold biased beliefs about women aren't evil people; rather, they're products of their upbringing and a lifetime of immersion in the swamp of hegemonic masculinity. The goal is not to punish them, but to create an atmosphere in which they can evolve their thinking in a natural way. Your Inclusion Institute's goal is not to point fingers and lay blame; it's to shine a light of empathy and understanding on bias and to make such a clear case in favor of dignity that moving toward it feels authentic, not forced.

As a leader, you began your journey toward dignity with Tool #1, when you took the meaningful steps of exploring and challenging your own biases. Creating an Inclusion Institute in your organization expands that commitment beyond yourself and to your fellow executives and employees.

The Human Library

One of the very best ways for people to develop empathy and challenge stereotypes is to have honest, real conversations with individuals who frequently experience bias and a lack of empathy. That's the thinking behind The Human Library, an international movement first launched in Copenhagen, Denmark, in 2000.[76] The goal of The Human Library is to break down bias and build up empathy by facilitating conversations between people who ordinarily might not have a reason to engage with each other.

Seeing, talking with, listening to, and being present with—in person—individuals whose life stories are entirely different than ours can dramatically expand our understanding of how they experience the world. Connecting with them through the heart is a powerful way to appreciate their challenges, strengths, and humanity, and to create a space in which empathy can grow. Engaging with a Human Library is very powerful for building empathy, because participants talk directly with someone who has suffered as a result of bias.

For some (but again, not all) straight white males who hold power in business, their experience with people who are other from them is quite limited. They may have had few or no meaningful, one-on-one conversations about bias with women, people of color, gay people, and others who are not like them. As a result, they may lack the ability to interact comfortably with members of those groups. Having an opportunity to talk with others and hear their stories in a safe, supportive space—through an organization's Human Library— gives participants the confidence to initiate conversations with diverse people in an organization. It can also strengthen their openness to being more intentional about bringing others into leadership circles, facilitating development attention, and creating mentorship or support relationships. All of the people in an organization—starting at the top with the board of directors, CEO, and leadership team—can benefit from participating in Human Library activities.

Here's how you can create a Human Library in your organization. Working with your human resources department, ask individuals from your community and your company to volunteer to share their stories with small groups of employees. You may also want to reach out to community groups to help connect you with populations that are not represented in your company, such as homeless individuals or undocumented workers. If your organization has overseas offices, take advantage of their visits to headquarters to promote cross-cultural relationship building. These in-person events can occur on a regular basis (ideally monthly or quarterly). You can also do them virtually or via video, but face-to-face interactions are so much more effective.

Virtual Reality to Bias-Busting Tools

In chapter 4 we looked at the ways in which the first-person perspective of video games such as Grand Theft Auto allows players to feel as if they, rather than the characters in the game, are performing the actions on the screen. In misogynistic gaming, this kind of virtual reality experience reinforces biased belief systems, because even though actions occur on screen, players' brains experience them as if they are reality.

Here's a way to turn that on its head. Your Inclusion Institute can make virtual reality a force for good, rather than bias, by taking advantage of applications and systems that use the on-screen feeling of first-person reality to demonstrate how it feels to experience bias. An approach known as virtual identity tourism uses technology for a good cause by helping people really understand what it is to be someone else.

Virtual reality is showing great promise as an empathy-building tool. In one study, researchers in Europe used virtual reality to alter subjects' own skin color. After seeing and interacting with their different-colored limbs, subjects took tests that reflected increases in their empathy levels.[77] And in a Stanford University study, participants who "experienced" via virtual reality what it would be like lose their jobs and homes developed longer-lasting compassion toward the homeless than those who were exposed to a homelessness narrative via text or other delivery methods. "Experiences are what define us as humans, so it's not surprising that an intense experience in VR is more impactful than imagining something," Jeremy Bailenson, a professor of communications and a co-researcher of the study, said in a Stanford News article.[78]

Recognizing the potential of virtual reality in reducing bias, forward-thinking companies are creating applications that could deserve a place in your Inclusion Institute. For example, the company Equal Reality offers virtual reality-based diversity and inclusion training that allows users to literally see from the point of view of others, including those of a different gender, race, or ability level.[79] Virtual reality allows users to feel the emotional impact of offensive words and actions on others, according to Annie Drake, co-founder of Equal Reality.[80] Using virtual reality goggles, specially designed software, and custom-tailored scenarios, Equal Reality makes bias feel real. "We're bringing the authenticity of the role-playing to a large scale, and … converting people who need to learn how to treat others better," Drake says.

Another great tech tool is a new Catalyst offering, #BiasCorrect, which is a plug-in designed to tag unconscious bias in real-time conversations on work-based chat platforms. "The plug-in identifies words that create harmful gender stereotypes and suggests alternative language," according to Catalyst. "For instance, if a woman is described as 'aggressive,' the app suggests correcting the sentiment to 'assertive.'" Eskalera, the company that developed the technology for the plug-in, is making the software available via open source code in an effort to spread the message of unconscious bias and to encourage change across every chat platform.[81]

Hopefully one day soon, this book will be updated to describe a virtual reality system that pushes back on women when they engage in thinking patterns that work against them. So few women have good female role models to learn from, and a VR tool to meet your confident self would be an amazing addition to an Inclusion Institute's learning tools.

Teaching Empathy as a Leadership Competency

In Part I of this book, we looked at the ways in which bias can infiltrate every part of our culture and outlook. Bias in film, social media, video games, and education continues to exist because misogyny has the power to strip away human empathy. Without empathy, which is the ability to sense and share another person's emotions and feelings, individuals can easily lose sight of how their words and actions affect others, especially those who have been marginalized by male hegemonic power or other biased belief systems. Empathy makes dignity possible.

Unfortunately, because of the negative impact of the hegemonic masculinity and misogyny, some (but certainly not all) men lack a strong sense of empathy for women and their experiences in life and in the workplace. Building up empathy is a crucial foundation for dignity and equity, and an imperative driving force for an Inclusion Institute. In fact, empathy is such an important capability that organizations committed to dignity and inclusion must think of it as a leadership competency that is as important as strategic acumen, financial literacy, and other crucial competencies.

As we've discussed, dignity is the belief that everyone in an organization has the same worth and the same fundamental human needs as everyone else. Having a well-developed sense of empathy allows people to put themselves in other people's shoes and to understand others' fundamental human needs in a very real way. The need to understand—and to be understood—is an absolutely essential ingredient to solving the problem of bias and inequity in the workplace and in the world.

Without empathy, men can't comprehend how their biased words and actions impact women. They don't understand why an insensitive text, a sexually explicit comment, an uninvited touch, or a whisper in a woman's ear would bother her. They don't realize why micro-aggressions have the power to undermine a woman's confidence. Empathy enables a man to understand how and why biased behaviors and micro-aggressions interfere with their dignity and job performance.

Just as there are assessment tests for bias, there are tests that measure empathy.

One of my favorites is the Empathy Quiz from the Greater Good Science Center at UC Berkeley.[82] It draws on three scientifically validated scales that researchers have created to measure empathy. The quiz can be found at https://greatergood.berkeley.edu/quizzes/take_quiz/empathy. Lower scores indicate a lower level of empathy and can be used to identify employees that require prioritization in empathy skills development. It's important to remember that the reason to identify low empathy levels in your employees is not to be punitive, but to recognize it as an area that needs development. Once it's acknowledged, it can be addressed using empathy-building tools in your Inclusion Institute.

The Foundation of Inclusion: Building Confidence

An Inclusion Institute has two audiences: The people who experience bias (in this book we're focusing on women, but in an organization, this includes members of all groups subject to prejudice and marginalization) and the men whose words and actions are driven by male hegemonic power myths. Some programs and learning opportunities are geared toward one of those audiences, but others are appropriate for both.

Because confidence issues and imposter syndrome are major roadblocks for so many women who have experienced bias, building confidence is a foundational goal in nearly all Inclusion Institute programming for women. We have discussed imposter syndrome and confidence issues elsewhere in this book, especially in Chapter 4. Confidence is the trust that a woman has in her abilities—for example, the ability to work a room during a networking event or to communicate strategic thinking. Imposter syndrome goes beyond confidence issues; it is an underestimation of the skills and abilities a woman possesses, and it carries with it a feeling that despite her education and experience, she's really not as accomplished as the evidence suggests. People who experience imposter syndrome— which primarily affects women, but also strikes men—believe they've somehow fooled others into believing that they possess intelligence or skills that they actually don't have, and that at any moment, they could be exposed as frauds.

Because confidence issues are fed by bias and the hegemonic masculinity that surrounds women their entire lives, learning strategies to build confidence belong in your organization's Inclusion Institute. These strategies should be directed in three ways:

1. To support women who struggle with confidence issues.
2. To redirect men whose words and behaviors undermine women's confidence.
3. To educate men to choose words and behaviors that create space for women to trust themselves and their abilities.

An effective way of supporting women who struggle with confidence issues is a training approach that is modeled after cognitive restructuring, a technique drawn from the psychological treatment known as cognitive behavioral therapy. Using cognitive restructuring, individuals learn to identify, challenge, and reframe cognitive distortions, which are thought patterns that cause them stress. Some of these unhelpful thinking patterns include all-or-nothing thinking ("If I don't do this report perfectly I'm a complete failure."), overgeneralizing ("Everyone is smarter than I am."), and disqualifying the positive ("Receiving a top score on my performance review doesn't mean I'm succeeding.").

Disqualifying the positive is an especially tenacious, prevalent thought pattern in women with imposter syndrome and confidence issues, especially after 360 feedback situations. Using a mental filter, they may ignore any positive feedback they receive and focus only on their "areas for development." This is such an enormous mistake, because research has shown repeatedly that our strengths lead us to success and focusing on positive feedback allows us to expand our strengths even further. Owning one's strengths is a critical step toward building confidence, so be sure your Inclusion Institute includes programs that provide training in cognitive restructuring and reframing automatic negative thoughts in a more positive, helpful way.

Confronting Micro-aggressions

Reducing women's exposure to micro-aggressions is an important way to create room for confidence growth. Micro-aggressions are words or actions that disrespect and discriminate against women in subtle or indirect ways. (Again, we're focusing on gender here, but these issues apply to all groups that experience bias.) Micro-aggressions can be intentional or not; they include slights and snubs, as well as insults. As their name (micro) suggests, these words and actions appear small when considered individually; most people would consider them less overtly objectionable than greater aggressions (such as sexual assault, for example). But that doesn't mean micro-aggressions are harmless. In fact, the damage of micro-aggressions adds up over time and can often be as detrimental as larger acts of aggression.

When micro-aggressions accumulate, they wear women down and chip away at their confidence. "Women who experience micro-aggressions view their workplaces as less fair and are three times more likely to regularly think about leaving their job than women who don't," according to Women in the Workplace 2018, a study undertaken by LeanIn.Org and McKinsey.[83] The study found that workplace micro-aggressions are a reality for 64% of women. Women of color tend to be subjected to even more micro-aggressions than white women; based on my own anecdotal research, I believe micro-aggressions are status quo for least 80% of women of color.

Not only do micro-aggressions contribute to confidence issues and imposter syndrome, but they interfere with women's ability to work with dignity. Remember, in addition to having the same worth, everyone in your organization has the same fundamental human needs; meeting these needs leads to psychological health. As we discussed earlier, the brilliant psychologist Abraham Maslow delineated those needs as physiological needs (air, water, food, shelter, sleep, etc.), safety needs, love and belonging, esteem (from one's self and from others), and self-actualization. Being subjected to micro-aggressions on a regular basis interferes with women's ability to have their fundamental needs met at work. When lower-level needs go unfilled, women have a reduced capacity to self-actualize; as we've discussed before, this not only harms women, but it can diminish their ability to perform at their highest level at work and to contribute fully to your organization. As such, eliminating micro-aggressions is an important step toward restoring dignity and facilitating the fulfillment of fundamental human needs.

The following chart shows some common micro-aggressions, along with the fundamental human needs they deny:

Micro-aggression Examples	Fundamental Needs Denied by This Micro-aggression
Sexual comments on appearance or dress Asking for a hug, touching a woman's hair, or other physical contact Staring at a woman's body Advances or comments with sexual innuendo, such as, "You're so gorgeous; you must drive your husband crazy" Sharing photos of a sexual nature Choosing to lay off a woman rather than a man because the man has a family to support Following a woman into an enclosed space, such as a supply closet	Shelter (because reporting the incident could lead to a loss of employment), safety, esteem, self-actualization

Invading a woman's personal space by standing too close to her	Safety
Failing to acknowledge a women's strategic or content-related contributions to the team or assignment	Safety, belonging, esteem, self-actualization
Asking a female staff member to make coffee or take notes	Safety, esteem, self-actualization
Carrying out last-minute efforts to create a surface-level appearance of equality and inclusion (e.g. rushing around the office to find more women to include in a team photo when the photographer points out the shot will include mostly/all men, finding one female panelist at the last minute to prevent hosting an all-male panel, etc.)	Esteem, self-actualization
Thoughtlessly using stereotypes like "aggressive," icy," or "cold" to describe female colleagues' behavior	Esteem, belonging, self-actualization
Assuming that women have better attention to detail, rather than understanding that attention to detail is a choice and a skill that can be learned by anyone. (This often has implications as "workplace housework" is assigned and/ or during recruitment for administrative support positions.)	Esteem, self-actualization
Asking illegal questions in a job interview (Are you married? Planning a family?)	Safety, esteem, self-actualization
A man ignoring or talking over women, or repeating a woman's idea as his own	Esteem, belonging, self-actualization

Mansplaining (for example, explaining to a woman the meaning of a sports analogy commonly used in business, interrupting a woman to summarize her thoughts for the group)	Esteem, belonging, self-actualization
Interrupting a woman while she speaks	Esteem, belonging, self-actualization
Alluding to a woman's hormone levels or menstrual cycle to explain her behavior	Safety, esteem, self-actualization
Shutting women out of informal information loops, leaving them off emails they need to receive, sabotaging their effectiveness	Safety (lack of trust), esteem, self-actualization
Excluding women from company travel/trips where important business and networking will take place	Safety (lack of trust), esteem, self-actualization
Making it impossible for women to participate in afterhours work because of scheduling conflicts or inappropriate venue	Safety (lack of trust), esteem, self-actualization
Making belittling comments such as, "What are you ladies chit-chatting about?" (The suggestion is that it couldn't possibly be about business.)	Esteem, belonging, self-actualization
Shaming women in front of their colleagues; for example, telling a woman she's not needed in client meetings	Safety (lack of trust), esteem, belonging, self-actualization

Exacerbating the discomfort of a woman when she's the only female in the group	Safety (lack of trust), esteem, belonging, self-actualization
Planning or failing to redirect activities such as long hours at the bar after work, ping pong tourneys when the women don't play (or don't play with testosterone-fueled intensity), hanging out at a hot tub in swimwear, going to male-focused off-sites (such as hunting trips), or planning retreats where women and men share bathrooms or close quarters	
Avoiding group bonding activities that would allow a woman to shine; for example, planning golf rather than a 5K because one of the women on the team was a collegiate track star	Esteem, belonging, self-actualization
Stepping back and letting a woman flounder when she's in the midst of a work crisis, rather than jumping in to help	Shelter, safety, belonging, esteem, self-actualization
Reaching over a female manager to build a connection with her male counterpart instead	Safety (trust), esteem, self-actualization
Creating independent relationships with a female manager's peers	Safety (trust), esteem, belonging, self-actualization

Learning experiences in an Inclusion Institute must be designed not only to enlighten men about the inappropriateness of these micro-aggressions, but to give them alternatives that reflect a Dignity Mindset.

Make a Baseline Bias Assessment

The best development always begins with an assessment to determine a learner's baseline. Once a baseline is defined and knowledge/skills gaps are identified, learning curriculum can target those gaps. Identifying bias is so important because when people are aware of their biases, they can make conscious choices to change them.

Similarly, a baseline assessment helps acknowledge the unconscious biases that must be addressed. It's important to recognize that all people have biases, as Catalyst has so eloquently pointed out: "Unconscious bias exists in each person's world view, affecting our behavior from the classroom to the workplace. We don't necessarily feel it, but many of those around us do. As a result, unconscious bias creates barriers to inclusion, performance, engagement, and, ultimately, innovation. And while we cannot completely rid ourselves of unconscious bias, learning how to mitigate its impact is a skill that everyone can learn."[84] These bias mitigation tools can be taught through an Inclusion Institute.

A great example of a baseline assessment tool for bias is the Implicit Association Tests developed by Project Implicit, which was founded by scientists from Harvard, the University of Washington, and the University of Virginia.[85] Project Implicit (www.projectimplicit.net) provides online assessment tests designed to identify bias related to gender, race, sexuality, age, disability, and other constructs.[86]

Although anyone can take the Project Implicit tests, some of the more dignity-grounded organizations are integrating them into leadership development programming and bringing in coaches to help participants learn from and create development goals around bias. There are other bias assessments, too; whichever ones you choose to use, be sure they give you an accurate baseline on bias, just as you would be sure to measure any other mission-critical competency before launching a training program to address it.

Debate Clubs for Women

Executive presence is a key leadership competency. Many programs and books explore methods for developing executive presence; however, based on my coaching work, I've come to understand it as comfortably commanding a space—something I also call "confident casual"—as simply the ability to confidently take and hold the floor. In combing through hundreds of coaching files, I realized that women who had debate training—as far back as high school but up to and including at law school—were more confident and more skilled at executive presence. So, the idea for your Institute is to create year-long women's debate clubs within your organization.

Learning to debate builds many skills that boost confidence and contribute to executive presence, including critical thinking, communication, creativity, and strength in public speaking. For the greatest impact, year-long women's debate club programs spearheaded by your Inclusion Institute and led by a professional with extensive debate experience should be held in person in each of your organization's locations.

Strategy Courses

You can help strengthen your employees' strategic thinking and communication skills with six-month strategy courses. These courses can benefit women (and men) for whom strategic thinking doesn't come naturally. This learning area is a need for some but not all women, because strategic thinking and communication can be a key sticking point for individuals with the potential to advance in an organization. Leaders must excel at contributing at a strategic level, but competency in this area doesn't necessarily match the number of years worked.

Unfortunately, strategy can be difficult to describe, let alone teach. I once coached an executive whose manager told her she needed to be more strategic. When she asked him what she would be doing if she was "being more strategic," he said, "You'd be doing your thinking." Still unclear, she asked, "Thinking about what?" and he said, "Strategy!" What a puzzle strategy is: Leaders all need it, but even those who practice it well may be hard pressed to explain it.

The solution to this puzzle is to bring in trainers with a deep knowledge of how best to approach the development of strategic thinking and communication. Consider offering an actual MBA-level course on strategy that uses the case method and requires participants to pass an exam on a case.

Sponsorship Programs for Developing Senior Leaders

Sponsorships pair high-potential women on the verge of moving into significant leadership roles at senior levels in the organization with senior leaders who are willing to take an active role in their development. Although sponsors are sometimes mentors (teachers), they go further, providing significant direct exposure and visibility to key decision makers in the core power structure. Sponsorships are an excellent way to prepare women to join an organization's power structure through shadowing, engaging with the sponsor's network, and receiving recommendations from the sponsor for next assignments at the end of the program, which typically lasts one year.

A sponsorship program should have a very high bar for enrollment, both for sponsors and those being sponsored. High-potential women can be identified via the succession planning process. A sponsorship program is not the place for organic connection and loose oversight; the best outcomes result from sponsorship programs that are carefully crafted and well managed with a goal of widening the pipeline of women moving from mid-level to senior-level to executive ranks.

Mentorship Programs for Developing Professionals

Like sponsorships, mentor programs should be carefully designed and conscientiously managed. Poorly directed mentorship programs often falter, either because mentors drop the ball or because of a lack of structure and accountability. Your Inclusion Institute can create mentorship program success by following these steps:

- **Ask for volunteers to become mentors.** Don't "voluntell" people that they are going to be a mentor. Effective mentors take on the responsibility because they believe in it. True volunteers show up with intention and enthusiasm; coerced volunteers can cause more harm than good.

+ **Use wisdom choosing mentees.** Identify truly high-performing and high-potential talent in the middle of the pipeline, including women of color, to pair with mentors.

+ **Build structure into the program.** Create an informal set of learning objectives that provide focus, as well as a plan for meeting frequency. Include one-on-one meetings and group events with multiple mentors and mentees.

+ **Have mentees shadow their mentors.** This is especially important for mentees who have been marginalized because of gender, race, and so on.

+ **Include networking events.** Informal networking events can be intimidating to women, people of color, and others who don't come from the traditional male power structure. Mentors can address this discomfort in mentees by accompanying them to informal networking events and encouraging them to meet and talk with participants. To raise comfort levels, mentors can work with mentees to prepare for these events well in advance.

+ **Set an end date for the pairing.** Six to 12 months is typically a good length for a mentorship.

+ **Seek input afterwards.** Feedback from both mentors and mentees can help make your program stronger.

Feedback Training for Managers

Useful, thoughtful feedback can help build confidence, especially in younger employees, new hires, and people who struggle with confidence issues and imposter syndrome. One of the simplest steps managers can take to reduce the anxiety that plagues so many employees is to give them specific feedback on how they're doing. Feedback should be given on an ongoing basis, at scheduled times and on an as-needed basis. Even brief feedback sessions provide value.

A pillar of your Inclusion Institute can be training for managers in successful feedback strategies. (See Dignity Mindset Tool #3: Communicate With Dignity by Mastering 7 Consequential Conversations for tips on how to give positive feedback and constructive feedback.) Successful feedback isn't just evaluative; it acknowledges jobs well done and offers specific learning on how to grow and successfully expand skill sets.

An Idea Whose Time Has Come

The suggestions included here are just a few examples of the ways in which you can populate your organization's Inclusion Institute. As with all laboratories of learning, the Inclusion Institute is envisioned as an adaptive and dynamic force for personal and professional growth, continuously evolving as it must to remain relevant.

Communicate with Dignity by Mastering Seven Consequential Conversations

"When you produce a thought that is full of understanding, forgiveness, and compassion, that thought will immediately have a healing effect on both your physical and mental health and on those around you. If you think a thought that is full of judgment and anger, that thought will immediately poison your body and mind and the people around you."

— Zen Master Thich Nhat Hanh, author of *The Art of Communicating*

Good communication is crucial to the success of any organization. However, it's especially important in a business in which a leader has committed to the intention of replacing biased belief systems with inclusive, dignity-based belief systems. Skillful leaders communicate their commitment to dignity through their actions and by modeling inclusivity; but that's not enough. To bring about significant change, you must have powerful communication skills that serve you as you seek to inspire your colleagues and employees to release bias and embrace dignity.

As you implement a Dignity Mindset in your organization, challenges will arise. That's to be expected. Rather than being surprised or thrown off challenges, however, you can take some important steps to prepare for them. Knowing how to communicate about conflict not only presents ways to defuse it but creates learning opportunities for everyone involved.

Unfortunately, most people lack the skills they need to communicate in a way that defuses or prevents conflict. As a result, rather than working through problems, people tend to respond to them in ways that make the situation worse. Employees may complain to their managers or the human resources department. Or they may just grumble and spread rumors about the person with whom they're in conflict. These types of responses are quite counterproductive. We want people talking to, not hiding from or sniping at one another.

The fear of conflict may prevent leaders from talking about gender or race—worried that you'll say something wrong, you may say nothing. But if you can't talk about it, how are you going to change it?

Be assured that the fear of making communications mistakes is quite common at every level of the organization. Fortunately, learning and practice can bring about dramatic improvements. Even if you're not a naturally brilliant communicator, you can pick up new skills quickly. With the right communication strategies in hand, you can tackle even the most challenging conversations with composure.

For this Dignity Mindset tool, I've turned to Alesia Latson, founder and CEO of Latson Leadership Group. Alesia is a brilliant speaker, executive coach, and international management consultant. A few years ago, during a break between sessions at a conference we were both attending, I asked her what the most important thing was that she had learned about organizations thus far. Her answer was that there were seven consequential conversations everyone should know how to have. Something suddenly clicked, and I knew this would be vital to the work of gender equity.

Knowing how to conduct these seven conversations will have a profound and positive impact on how you talk with the people in your organization about dignity, diversity, and inclusion. In each, you will see how dignity-based behaviors—shelter, safety, esteem, belongingness—are on the line, and how you and your managers can increase trust and engagement by handling them well.

Alesia's Seven Consequential Conversations are all built on one very important foundation: the idea that it's better to "call someone in" rather than to "call them out." In other words, when someone makes a mistake or says the wrong thing, rather than shaming them and calling *out* their behavior or words, call them *in* to a dialogue that allows you to bridge your issues, build trust, hold a space for learning, and create solutions. Applying the "call me in, don't call me out" foundation to gender (and race) is especially helpful because so often people offend others without even realizing it. Building bridges is a much better approach than eliciting shame.

Read on for a master class from my brilliant colleague that shows you how to successfully conduct the consequential conversations that can help steer your organization toward dignity.

Conversation 1: Giving Positive Feedback

Positive feedback can be a critical element in replacing bias with dignity. When you give positive feedback, you let your colleagues and employees know that you notice, appreciate, and support their efforts to embrace a Dignity Mindset. It boosts others' self-esteem and has the potential to enhance their attitude toward you, their colleagues, their work, and the organization.

You can maximize the impact of positive feedback by making it immediate, specific, impactful, encouraging, and focused. Do so by following these five steps, which we'll examine within the framework of a conversation between you and Rick, one of the people on your team.

1. **Give a head's up.** When you state the purpose of your conversation, you allow your listener to be open to what you're about to say.
2. **Share your observations.** Be objective, brief, specific, and descriptive—don't just say "great job!" Make it a "verbal video" that's like a play-by-play.
3. **State the impact or consequences of the action.** Explain how it affects you, your team, or your organization.
4. **Acknowledge effort and express appreciation.**
5. **Ask for reaction with an open-ended question.** This is optional— do it if it makes sense.

Here's how a conversation might look when you give positive feedback to Rick regarding the way he supported Jasmine, a new team member and the only woman at the meeting.

"Rick, I have some observations I'd like to share about what you did well during today's meeting. *(head's up)* Here's what stood out for me about that interaction. When Jasmine was giving her recommendations about next steps, Bob interrupted her, and you intervened on her behalf in a gracious way that was helpful to Jasmine and polite to Bob. You told Bob that you thought we should hear all of Jasmine's ideas before any of us commented on them. *(share your observations)* What I noticed after that was that Jasmine seemed more self-assured—her eye contact was steady and direct, she offered her recommendations resolutely, and Bob waited for her to finish before saying anything else.

And I think everyone in the room appreciated your advocating for a new team member. *(impact)* Thank you—I really appreciate the effort you put into supporting Jasmine and representing our team in such a positive way. *(appreciation)* What was your take on the meeting? *(reaction)*"

By giving positive feedback in an effective way, you not only recognize and reinforce Rick's exceptional behavior, but you let him know you're paying attention. And you help build support for Jasmine.

Conversation 2: Giving Constructive Feedback

It's no fun, but as a leader, it's your job to give constructive feedback when needed. It's a useful way to redirect problem performance, and it sets expectations for future behaviors.

Constructive feedback is a powerful tool for changing biased behavior.

Don't think of constructive feedback as punishment, but as a way to bring about improvements and to let people know you're on their side, even when they make mistakes.

Your goal with constructive feedback is to be helpful, rather than punitive.

As with positive feedback, constructive feedback is most useful when it is specific, timely, focused, impactful, and encouraging. To do it effectively, follow these steps, which we'll examine within the framework of a conversation with Bob, the team member who interrupted Jasmine in the previous example.

1. **Give a head's up** and check in on the recipient's willingness to receive it. (Asking if now is a good time to talk gives the recipient of the feedback some power.)
2. **Share your observations.** Do so in an objective, neutral way.
3. **State the impact or consequences of the action.** Explain how it affects you, your team, or your organization.
4. **Check in.** Ask an open-ended question to learn the other person's perspective and intention.
5. **Paraphrase.** Repeat back what the person says to show she or he is being heard and ask if you've got it right.
6. **Ask for a change in action.** What can the person do differently in the future?
7. **Check for a commitment to change in the future.**
8. **Express appreciation.**

Here's how your conversation with Bob might go:

"Bob, I'd like to share some observations about what I noticed in the interaction between you and Jasmine during today's meeting, and I'd like to talk about some possible upgrades for the future. Is now a good time for you?" *(head's up)* During the meeting, while Jasmine was making her presentation, you began to share your thoughts before she had an opportunity to finish what she was saying. I noticed that you spoke to her in a tone that in my mind varied from your usual pleasant manner. *(share your observations— notice you don't use the word "interrupt" which is judgmental and might put Bob on the defensive)* I saw that when this happened, Jasmine lost her train of thought while she was making what I thought was a particularly salient point. *(impact)* Bob, let me check in with you on this— what was going on for you at this point? *(check in; give Bob time to respond)* Bob, what I hear you saying is that you didn't mean to interrupt Jasmine, but you felt that she was taking too long to make her point, so you thought that if you made a comment it might move things along. Do I have that right? *(paraphrase)* Bob, how can you handle this differently if it happens again in the future? *(ask for a change in action, and give Bob time to respond)* So we've agreed that in the future you'll let other team members complete their presentations before making your comments, and that you'll write down your thoughts in your notes so you don't forget any of them? *(check for a commitment to change)* Thanks for your openness and for having this conversation with me, Bob! *(appreciation)*"

Of course, if deeper issues arise during your conversation with Bob, you'll need to address them. If so, aim to keep the conversation neutral, focusing on reflecting back a play-by-play of Bob's actions rather than making judgments about him or his behaviors. Paraphrase his comments back to him so he knows he's being heard; encourage him to propose suggested actions for the future rather than imposing your recommendations on him. (Sometimes you will have to impose, but solutions are always better when they come from the person who's responsible for implementing them.) Above all, aim to maintain a friendly tone, so Bob feels supported rather than judged. Your goal is to train new behaviors, not to make Bob feel attacked and defensive.

Conversation 3: Asking for Feedback

Asking for feedback benefits leaders in a few ways. It gives you information about your words and actions that you can use to grow and improve. It also shows your team that you value their thoughts and wisdom—you don't think of yourself as the person with all the answers.

Being able to ask for and benefit from feedback is important as you adapt a Dignity Mindset and restructure biased belief systems, because it gives you the opportunity to learn from people in your organization who are "other" than you. And if you solicit feedback in an effective way, you have the potential to build crucial bridges with people who may feel marginalized. For example, if you're a man who's working on making women feel more welcome on your team, asking them for feedback—either about business-related issues or about your efforts to increase inclusion—can benefit you and the women to whom you reach out for feedback.

When you ask for feedback, be as specific as possible about what you're curious to know. The more specific you can be, the better. It's hard for people to give feedback without context, especially if there's a status differential—if you're a manager and you're speaking to someone who reports to you, for instance. Unless you are specific, that person doesn't know if you really do want honest feedback or you're fishing for compliments. You want to make it easy for people to tell you the truth. You also want to prepare yourself to receive feedback before seeking it by taking a few deep breaths and reminding yourself that asking for feedback requires courage and vulnerability.

Here's how you might start a conversation with Daphne, a woman on your team, about your efforts to be more inclusive in meetings. After checking in with her to see if she'd be willing to give you feedback, and making sure that now is a good time to make the request, you might say something like this:

"Daphne, I have some concerns that I'm not being as inclusive during meetings as I could be—that I may miss opportunities to invite people to participate. This is something that I've been working on, and I'd love to get your observations about how I'm doing. I'd like to know what you've noticed about how inclusive I am, what I'm doing well, and what opportunities I may be missing. Where would you give me some coaching?"

By being very clear about what you're requesting, you create an opportunity for Daphne to offer responses that truly are helpful to you. As she does, listen carefully and with an open mind. After Daphne offers a response, ask, "What else?" to hold a space for her to expand on her feedback. Focus attentively as she speaks and allow her to explain herself without interruption.

After you've received your feedback from Daphne, summarize it back to her to make sure you understand her and to show her you've listened carefully. Then thank her. And acknowledge yourself for having done something difficult. Asking for honest feedback isn't easy and doing so can surface your threat response. But feedback can be a powerful teacher, so it's worthwhile to seek it.

Conversation 4: Making Requests

The best way to increase your likelihood of getting your needs met is to make a direct request. It's important for you to be precise when you make a request so that the person to whom you're addressing your query can understand exactly what you're looking for and why it matters to you.

Before making a request, spend some time thinking about exactly what outcome you seek. Too often, requests become sources of conflict because the person who's making the ask doesn't really know what they want. To have this conversation in a successful way, follow these four steps:

1. **Give a head's up.** Alert the person that you're making a request.
2. **State your request clearly and succinctly.**
3. **Share the value, benefit, or consideration around the request.** In other words, give the reason for the request, what positives will come from it, and what difficulties may have to be negotiated in order for the request to be fulfilled.
4. **Ask for reaction.** Use an open-ended question to give the other person space to discuss it with you.

Here's how you might make a request of Steve, a hiring manager on your team. You'd like Steve to take steps to expand his recruitment efforts to include more women candidates for the position of chief engineer in your organization. After checking in with Steve to make sure now is a good time to talk, you might say something like this:

"Steve, I'd like to make a request. (*head's up*) I would like us to broaden our search for the chief engineer position so that our applicant pool is at least 50% women. (*state your request*) Here's why I'm adamant about this: Hiring more women is consistent with our commitment to inclusion, and as you know our research shows that having greater diversity can have a positive impact on our company's performance in the market. Now, I know that expanding the applicant pool to include 50% women could extend our timeline for the search, but I think it's important enough for us to adjust the timeline. (*share the value, benefit, or consideration*) What are your thoughts about this, Steve? (*reaction*)"

After asking Steve this open-ended question, follow with complete silence and allow Steve the space to answer. (It's important to point out that at this point many people— particularly women—don't wait for an answer; instead they jump in either to provide answers for themselves or to walk back the request. Don't do that.)

Ideally, Steve will agree to your request and you'll work on a plan to recruit more women for the open position. But Steve may push back and give you a list of reasons that he feels your request is unreasonable. When that happens, have the next conversation.

Conversation 5: Gaining Agreement

Let's continue with the conversation between you and Steve about expanding the applicant pool for the chief engineering position to include 50% women. You've made your case, and Steve shuts you down.

To move towards agreement, rather than having the conversation spiral into a disagreement, bring things to a neutral place by summarizing Steve's points back to him. This shows you're listening carefully. Say something like this: "Steve, what I hear you saying is that identifying a 50% female applicant pool will take too long. It's an engineering position, and you feel that the department needs to have the top position filled sooner rather than later. You're also saying that it can be challenging to find women in the STEM space, and you see this as something you really can't do right now. Is that right?"

Assuming you've summarized Steve's comments accurately, he'll say, "Yes. You've got that right."

This is a very important "yes."

In a conversation that turns into a conflict, this is often the point that the conflict spiral starts. Instead of calmly repeating back Steve's position, you might restate yours, and he might restate his, and before you know it you're both stuck in a place where you're each so intent on defending your own position that you can't open up to the other person's view. But when you summarize Steve's position without judgment and he confirms that you've summarized it correctly, you're on neutral ground.

Your next step is to ask Steve an open-ended question that will help move the conversation forward: "Steve, based on what you just shared, here's my question: How can we have some urgency about filling this position and at the same time stay true to our organization's commitment to expand our pool of diversity candidates for engineering jobs? How can we achieve both of those objectives?"

Again, follow your question with complete silence and allow Steve the space to answer.

Chances are, Steve will propose a viable solution. For example, he might say, "Well, I suppose we can hire a recruiting agency rather than spearhead the hiring in-house. If you could free up some budget for this, we might be able to expand the pool in a timely way."

What's happened here is that instead of nudging Steve to argue with you, you've given him a space to think creatively. That's real progress.

Ordinarily it takes some back-and-forth to get to a resolution. If this happens, use open-ended questions to continue to explore Steve's concerns; each time, reflect them back to him and ask him to propose a solution that moves the conversation forward. This process helps create possibilities that go beyond what either you or Steve might come up with on your own. If you both keep at it in a spirit of cooperation, you're likely to reach a place of agreement without devolving into conflict and argument.

Conversation 6: Making an Apology

You don't have to look far to find examples of terrible apologies. Read any newspaper article or news feed and you'll find business leaders, politicians, and celebrities offering woefully inadequate apologies. Saying, "I'm sorry *if* you felt uncomfortable with anything I *might* have done," is not an apology.

Bad apologies erode trust and make situations worse; good, sincere apologies build trust. That's why it's important to know how to apologize well. Each one of us makes mistakes; it's part of being human. But knowing how to apologize effectively is an uncommon skill. Fortunately, you can learn how to do it well even if it doesn't come naturally to you.

When you stray from your values—as we all do sometimes—you lose integrity. But when you make an apology, you step forward to reclaim some of the integrity you lost when you committed the offense. You also have the opportunity to make a promise to the other person and to rebuild trust. Apologizing well requires courage, but when done properly, it can offer substantial rewards to both sides.

To explain how best to apologize, let's use an example in which you lose your temper during a meeting with Nia, one of the women on your team. Nia disagrees with one of your proposals, and when she calmly shares her doubts in a meeting, you lose your temper and lash out at her in a way that does not reflect your best self. After the meeting, you realize that you owe her an apology, so you make your way to her office. Here's what you might say:

"Nia, do you have a minute? I just want to check in about the interaction we just had." (If Nia says yes, proceed with your apology.) "Nia, I just want to say, my behavior in that meeting was completely unacceptable. I wish I could tell you I have an excuse for it, but I don't. I just lost it. I know I stepped over the line. Being more open to disagreement with my proposals is something I've been working on, but obviously I have more work to do in this area. I'm very sorry I spoke to you that way."

Now it's your turn to listen. Nia may accept your apology, or she may explain herself. Give her space to say her piece.

So that's the first part of a good apology. The second part is even more important, because it creates expectations for the future. After acknowledging what you did wrong, make a promise. "Nia, here's what you can count on from me moving forward. I promise that I will show you respect, and I'll manage myself in a way that will allow you to see me as being present and open to you even when we have a disagreement."

Including a promise is crucial in apologies because it offers reassurance that you will do your best not to let the same kind of behavior occur again in the future. It tells others that you're not only taking responsibility for what happened today, but that you are owning your future actions, too.

Be sure you're making a promise you can keep. For example, perhaps you're apologizing for arriving late to a meeting. If you struggle with time management, don't promise that you'll never be late again—that's just not realistic, and it's not a guarantee you can keep. Instead, promise that you will try your best to get to meetings on time, but if you do run late, you promise to call so that the other person is never left waiting and wondering where you are. That's a promise you are more likely to be able to honor.

Apologies are necessary because of imperfections; however, managing your imperfections skillfully can build trust. As you probably know, customer loyalty studies find that customers are more loyal *after* a breakdown that gets resolved in a constructive way than they are if there wasn't a breakdown in the first place. Having something go wrong and repaired in a positive way is how we form trust. Think of your conflict with Nia: If you apologize well and keep the promise you make to her, Nia's trust and loyalty will grow stronger than it would have been if you hadn't had a problem in the first place. Each time Nia sees you working diligently to keep your promise to her, she sees evidence that she can count on you to follow through on your commitments.

Apologies are crucial when people make gender-related mistakes in the workplace. Offering a sincere apology with a promise tells others that although you won't always get it right, you hold yourself open to their input when you do get it wrong. A sincere acknowledgment/promise apology tells others that they can trust you—perhaps not always to say the right thing, but always to own what you say and to receive the feedback that will help you get it right next time.

Conversation 7: Introducing Change

Change is difficult, and people often need evidence that it will benefit them. The status quo can be a very comfortable place, and when considering change, people tend to emphasize their worries about it before considering the benefits it could bring about. To persuade others to accept change, lead with the problem, not the solution. If you can establish a solid business case that highlights a problem, the change that can solve it is more palatable.

When having a conversation that introduces change, use a past, present, and future framework. Here's an example of a conversation you might have with your team about introducing greater gender balance on your team:

Start with the past: "In the past year, our team in its current configuration has accomplished so much that we can be excited about. We've begun to turn the corner on increasing sales, we're seeing some early progress in reducing customer service problems, and we have set goals in terms of building brand awareness and market share. We're off to a good start together to move our company forward, and I'm so proud of that." As you delineate past achievements, everyone in the room should be nodding their heads, because yes, the team has done so much! Thinking about wins puts them in a positive, open place.

Now, talk about the present: "So here's what's going on now. Our team is 95% male. Research is showing us that gender-balanced teams are more productive and have higher sales and profits than male-dominated teams.

Also, we're seeing that companies with gender balance are perceived as better places to work and attract a higher caliber of talent in their candidate pool. Our company dropped in the recent national "Best Places to Work" rankings, and according to HR, our applicant profiles are noticeably weaker than they have been in the past because of concerns about diversity. That leads me to conclude that our current configuration and gender imbalance could be impacting our ability to succeed moving forward.

Next, address the future: "Imagine what could happen if we don't make adjustments to our gender balance. Envision the impact it could have on our sales, productivity, the quality of our talent pool, and our rankings as a great place to work." If you're compelling enough, your team will be nodding in agreement as you make this business case for change.

Share a compelling vision: Once you've described the problem, move on to change you are introducing. "Here's my vision for addressing this issue. I envision us all being role models for gender equity not only within our organization, but for other companies in our market, as well. We can be vanguards in our commitment to gender equity while taking steps that will lead to greater organizational success."

Now propose a simple first step: "I propose that we take a simple first step by convening an off-site to take a closer look at gender equity, how it can benefit our company, and how we can go about evening things up." Remember, this first step has to be something that feels do-able without being threatening. People need space to process and adjust to what you're proposing.

Finally, address the cost of change: "I would be remiss if I didn't also admit that this may disrupt some of what we already have in place. I acknowledge that. The dynamics of our team could change as we add new people, and some of our roles could shift. But I promise we will look for the best solutions to those concerns as we work together." Notice that as you acknowledge disruptions, you're not offering solutions right now; but you are committing to finding solutions in the future. There's power in that kind of acknowledgment because you are signaling that you have stakeholders' best interests at heart.

Obviously, many discussions will follow as you set out to balance the ranks in your organization. But getting that first conversation right by starting with the problem and outlining the solution, rather than just jumping in with a major change that lacks context, sets the tone for openness during the process that follows.

Building Conversational Skills

There you have some very practical strategies for conducting seven consequential conversations that are likely to arise as you lead your organization with a Dignity Mindset, and as you seek to increase inclusion and diversity on your staff. None of it is rocket science, but many of these strategies don't come naturally. By being intentional and learning and practicing smart conversation strategies, you can skillfully navigate and facilitate potentially challenging conversations.

Thanks again to Alesia Latson, founder and CEO of Latson Leadership Group, for sharing the conversational wisdom included in this tool.

Use Dignity-Driven Talent Acquisition Approaches

"Diversity strengthens our innovative capacity, unleashes the potential of [our]employees, and thereby directly contributes to our business success."

— Janina Kugel, human resources board member
and chief diversity officer, Siemens

Back in 1977, renowned leadership expert Rosabeth Moss Kanter pointed out in her landmark book, *Men and Women of the Corporation*, that in corporate America, like hires like. In other words, the straight white men running the core power structure in most organizations were, in a sense, cloning themselves by hiring other straight white men just like them. According to Kanter, this style of hiring creates exclusive management circles that are closed to outsiders such as women.[87] She highlighted the tendency of male executives to reproduce their own, rather than bring in any type of other, as just one of many barriers preventing women from entering the professional ranks in business.

Unfortunately, things haven't changed so very much in the four-plus decades since Kanter made this observation. Like is still hiring like. Female CEOs in the U.S. are still astonishingly rare; as of May 2018, only 24 of the CEOs of Fortune 500 companies—just 4.8%—were women.[88] And, after reaching an all-time high of 32 in 2017, the number of Fortune 500 female CEOs actually *dropped* 25%, to 24, between 2017 and 2018. Why, when there is ample evidence that diversity drives organizational success,

125

are we still struggling to get more women into leadership roles? Simple: Because the go-to habit for executives hiring new talent is to tap into their own networks. And since many executives' networks are filled with people just like them, that's who they tend to recruit and hire. The straight white males in the existing core power structure have networks made up primarily of other straight white males—from their colleges, their country clubs, their kids' private schools' board of directors, the cultural organizations and nonprofit groups they serve, the fundraisers they attend, and so on. This isn't the result of some kind of nefarious plot—it's normal that an individual's formal and informal social groups consist of people who are a lot like them. But it becomes problematic when leaders reach primarily into their own narrow networks to source talent for a corporate team.

I've often heard male executives say they don't hire more women because they can't find qualified female talent. Of course, they can't, if they look only within their own networks. Perhaps the most notorious example of this came during a 2012 presidential debate, when candidate Mitt Romney was asked about pay equity. "I had the chance to pull together a cabinet [as governor of Massachusetts], and all the applicants seemed to be men," Romney said. "I went to a number of women's groups and said, 'Can you help us find folks?' And they brought us whole binders full of women."[89]

It's easy to laugh at this, but hey—at least Romney was trying.

To bring more talented women onto your team, you don't need Romney's binders full of women. What you do need, however, is to recognize that if your current recruiting strategies aren't leading to greater diversity within your organization, you need to find new recruiting strategies. If insanity is doing the same thing, over and over again, but expecting different results, then sticking with non-diverse hiring tactics to bring more women into your organization is just plain crazy.

The good news is that there are plenty of innovative approaches to talent acquisition that you can tap into to boost gender diversity and other inclusion goals in your company. These methods reflect a Dignity Mindset as well as a willingness to go beyond standard hiring strategies.

In this section, we'll explore some examples of effective strategies for increasing diversity in your organization's recruiting and hiring practices—not just to bring more women onto your team, which is our focus in this book, but also more diversity in terms of color, sexual orientation, cultural background, age, and physical ability as well.

Diverse Talent Brings Greater Financial Performance

Before we look at tactics, here's an important reminder: Increasing diversity isn't just the right thing to do—it's also the best thing for your company. Without a doubt, diversity at every level of an organization leads to improved performance and organizational success.

Diversity can be a significant source of both competitive advantage and financial strength for your organization.

Documentation of this advantage comes from a variety of sources. For example, in 2018 McKinsey & Company reported that companies in the top quartile for gender diversity on their executive teams were 21% percent more likely to experience above-average profitability than companies in the bottom quartile.[90] "Our research confirms that gender, ethnic, and cultural diversity, particularly within executive teams, continue to be correlated to financial performance across multiple countries worldwide," McKinsey reported.

Despite findings such as these, and despite the fact that many organizations say they have made a serious commitment to diverse hiring, we have a long way to go on gender diversity in hiring, according to another McKinsey report, "Women in the Workplace 2018." This report found that leadership in and upper management in corporate America breaks down in this way:

- 68% white males
- 19% white females
- 9% males of color
- 4% females of color[91]

Companies need to take decisive action to increase gender diversity and must double down on their efforts to bring more women into organizations, McKinsey says. "This starts with treating gender diversity like the business priority it is, from setting targets to holding leaders accountable for results. It requires closing gender gaps in hiring and promotions, especially early in the pipeline when women are most often overlooked. And it means taking bolder steps to create respectful and inclusive workplaces."[92]

Bolder Steps

So what are some of the bolder steps that business leaders can take to close gender gaps and hire more women? The first is to open up networks. If you're stuck in a "like hires like" habit, now's the time to break out of it.

In many organizations, people responsible for bringing in new talent—hiring managers, recruiters, and search firms, as well as company leadership—must work harder to expand their reach in the talent pool. There are so many other vibrant, diverse networks of extraordinary talent aside from straight white men. But organizations need creative matchmakers and innovative recruiting strategies to lead them to the talented, diverse individuals outside the same-old warmed up network.

To open up hiring networks to full diversity, CEOs must insist that all parties (internal and external) involved in their organization's talent acquisition roles use every available tool and technology to identify talented women. A simple way of getting started with this is to work with female recruiters. According to data from Scout Exchange, a platform for marketplace recruiting that I'll talk more about momentarily, engaging female recruiters is a highly effective way to improve gender equity in talent acquisition. Scout's analysis[93] found the following when comparing female and male recruiters:

+ Female recruiters are 130% more effective at getting female candidates hired.
+ Female recruiters are 25% more likely to submit female candidates for job openings.
+ Female recruiters achieve 43% higher candidate fill rates across job categories.

"Female recruiters are clearly more effective at finding and hiring female candidates, which makes them a competitive advantage for employers in any organization," says Ken Lazarus, CEO of Scout. "It also presents a potential opportunity for male recruiters to learn from them and become equally as successful."[94] It's amazing to think that taking a step as simple as working with female recruiters can be so potentially fruitful.

Faces of Diversity

When seeking to increase inclusivity in hiring, employers must highlight current female employees, "particularly those in leadership positions, as they may serve as role models for female applicants," suggests "Gender Insights Report: How Women Find Jobs Differently," a 2019 report from LinkedIn.[95]

This is an important point. When it comes to pursuing opportunities, some women need more encouragement than men, in part because there are so few role models to lead the way. This isn't surprising, when you think back to the male hegemonic belief systems that surround women beginning at birth. All of the influences we discussed in the earlier part of this book—toxic masculinity in our culture, the male gaze in the media, the gender bias baked into many video games, the negative impact of social media on girls and young women, and the anti-female bro culture on most college campuses—predisposes many women to lack confidence when it comes to job-hunting.

It's no surprise that the LinkedIn report on gender equity in workplaces, which the company created after analyzing billions of interactions between professionals, organizations, and recruiters, found that women are more likely than men to self-select *out* of job listings. Although both genders view LinkedIn job postings in similar numbers, the report found, women are 16% less likely than men to apply to a job after viewing it, and women apply to 20% fewer jobs than men.

I've seen this many times while coaching corporate leaders. Overall, women have less confidence than men when it comes to pursuing job opportunities, especially those on the higher rungs of the corporate ladder. That confidence gap continues through the job search process; Scout's data has re-confirmed a well-understood fact that most but not all men are more likely to *overstate* their qualifications, and most but not all women are more likely to *understate* them.

One of the things that stands in the way of women going after jobs is long lists of requirements in job descriptions. Overall, women take these requirement lists more seriously than men—something I've seen in my interactions with my clients, and data from both Scout and LinkedIn backs this up. Scout has found that women will apply to a job if they meet 80% of the criteria listed for the role, but men will apply if they meet only 40% of listed criteria.[96]

"Roles with endless lists of requirements, nice-to-haves, and strict seniority demands can deter women from applying, as they often want to make sure they check every box you list," the report says. So here's another simple way to attract more women to job openings in your organization: List the most important requirements, but don't create an exhaustive list. Keep it short.

The good news, according to LinkedIn, is that when women do apply to a job, they are 16% more likely than men to get hired—and 18% more likely to receive an offer if the role is more senior than their current position. "Given women's higher likelihood to get hired once they apply," says LinkedIn, we see strong reinforcement for the often-discussed but less often-executed tactic of building gender balance by adding more women to the pipeline.

Talented, experienced women are out there. Make some changes to your recruiting strategies, and you'll find them.

AI and Recruiting

Several companies are using artificial intelligence to improve diversity recruiting. One that has impressed me is Scout Exchange, a Boston-based firm that is on the forefront of gender inclusion in hiring. Scout uses big data to analyze patterns of hiring success. As the company describes it, Scout is a platform for marketplace recruiting that provides an innovative way to connect employers with the recruiters that can best help them find the talent they seek—recruiters who are most likely to be successful in filling an organization's specific job postings.

Scout uses machine learning to analyze billions of recruiting performance data points from thousands of recruiters in its marketplace;

this analysis allows the company to predict recruiter success by specific job type. Scout's AI then matches specific recruiters to specific jobs to ensure candidate quality while reducing fill times.[97] By taking a large range of data points from the job posting, the posting goes to preferred and pre-approved search firms but also to many other marketplace vendors beyond the usual suspects. Curating the best recruiters for each job allows Scout to ensure higher quality, more diverse candidates, and faster time to fill.

One of the things that really stands out with Scout is that its platform helps establish a relationship between employers and search firms that allows both to hold each other accountable for diversity and inclusivity.

Scout also uses machine learning to help reduce human decision bias in the recruiting industry. This goes back to the invisible bias we've discussed before—most people don't even see their own bias, because it's been cooked into them since birth by the male hegemonic power system. When recruiters and hiring managers can become more aware of their unconscious bias, they can replace those straight white male mindsets with more inclusive, dignity-based outlooks.

With its access to so much data and its connection with large networks of recruiters, Scout is in a unique position to identify and point out trends in hiring. For example, Scout noticed a spike in female executive hires after #MeToo; however, surveys also found that hires have since returned to pre-#MeToo levels, unfortunately.

Whether you rely on your internal hiring team to seek talent, external recruiters and placement companies, or a mix of both, be sure they know that diversity is a top priority for your organization. I have met a number of small-shop recruiters who to my great surprise didn't have gender equity anywhere in their priorities. Make sure recruiters have powerful strategies in place to attract diverse job candidates.

The Interview

When it comes to diverse job candidates, it makes sense for you to imagine yourself in their shoes during the interview process. What do they see, hear, and experience when they come to your office? What might jump out at them as being tone-deaf or lacking in dignity? For example, while visiting a business recently, I walked down a hallway lined with photographs of noteworthy executives from the company's history, and the vast majority of them were white men. This kind of imaging suggests all kinds of messages that go against your dignity and diversity goals. For a woman candidate, walking past that wall of fame does not convey a contemporary, diverse mindset. Already the female candidate feels like an outsider, and it's not a great way to start an interview. There is, unquestionably, the right place and space to honor the legacy of your organization's leaders. That's very important. But using your empathy, think of how you would feel if you walked down the hallway to the interview and none of the photos on the wall were like you in any way. You would feel like a guest, not a member, of the company. This feeling of being an outsider may be all you need to cross a company off your list and continue looking for an organization in which you feel more welcome.

Once the interview gets under way, be sure your people are prepared to answer questions about diversity from female job applicants. Women want to know that commitment to gender diversity is a company's core value, not just a pose the company is taking to appear diverse. Because you can't expect your hiring team to do something you can't do, put yourself to the test by imagining how you would answer questions about gender equality from a job candidate.

Ursula Mead, founder and CEO of InHerSight, an anonymous company ratings platform tailored specifically to women, recommends that job candidates ask hiring managers five questions[98] to find out where the organization stands on gender issues. These questions are designed for female job seekers, but they're excellent questions for hiring managers and dignity-focused leaders to ask themselves:

1. What would you tell women job candidates about why it's so great to work here?
2. Can you share data on your company's diversity?
3. Do company execs support your diversity efforts?
4. What diversity, inclusion, and cultural competence trainings have your managers had?
5. How are your recruiting efforts building a diverse workforce?

How did you do with those questions? Did you struggle with any of them? If so, you have an idea of where you might need to focus attention as you expand your company's diversity hiring skill sets. You might also want to try your answers out on women, to see if your empathy carried you over into the shoes of the other.

Hold Colleges Accountable

Your organization's hiring strategy may also include recruiting from university or business schools that are putting their students forward for campus interviews. Colleges are essential feeder pools of talent for many companies. If you recruit from colleges, you are in a powerful position to motivate them to operate within the framework of a Dignity Mindset.

As noted earlier in this book, there are many links between the collegiate experience and gender bias and sexual harassment. Many colleges do a poor job of keeping women safe on campus, failing to set high standards for the treatment of women and the behavior of men. There are exceptions, of course, but overall there is tremendous room for improvement in terms of prioritizing inclusion in classes, eliminating gender-based pay gaps among faculty, and confronting sexual assault on campus. And as we've seen in a number of high-profile incidents, too many colleges are willing to let male students off the hook with a "boys will be boys" response to incidents of sexual harassment on campus.

As a hiring organization, you can use your clout to help change the way women experience college and to hold colleges accountable for their commitment to dignity and diversity.

Your company can help reverse the male hegemonic power dynamic on college campuses by letting schools know that how women are treated on their watch matters to you, and that you're taking it into account when deciding whether to work with their career offices. You have leverage, because you have the jobs that their graduates want. The extent to which a company hires graduates from any particular college or university adds significantly to the value of that school and is highlighted in campus recruiting efforts.

Use both carrots and sticks: Seek out schools with track records that reflect a commitment to dignity and inclusion. Notify colleges that fail women that you will withhold your recruiting efforts if they don't clean up their acts. Let college career officers and administrators know that your presence at their career fairs or interview days is conditional based on their performance as dignity-based institutions. Before agreeing to network with or interview a college's students, ask questions such as:

- What is your college's commitment to diversity, inclusion, and dignity?
- What is your school doing to improve campus safety for women?
- What are you measuring and reporting regarding campus assault of women?
- What is your school's track record when it comes to teaching inclusion and unconscious bias as core curriculum? Are these classes required or optional?
- Have there been any major incidents on campus this year centered around race, gender, or sexual preference? If so, what were they, and what was done about them?
- What is your track record for gender equity among tenured faculty? Among adjunct and part-time instructors?
- What steps are you taking to hire and promote more women faculty?
- Do you have a pay gap for faculty based on race or gender? If so, what is it? What steps are you taking to close pay gaps?

The purpose of applying pressure as described above is to incent colleges and universities to do a much better job of starting the unlearning of bias, taking at least some of the burden off employers who are committed to operating with a Dignity Mindset. At present, the burden is being passed to you.

And remember, as you consider which colleges you want to work with, be prepared to do some deep digging to learn about their commitment to dignity, inclusion, and women's safety on campus. Some colleges may put more effort into making highly visible demonstrations of diversity than actually changing deep-seated but less visible injustices.

An example of this is commencement speakers. GenderAvenger, a wonderful volunteer organization dedicated to ensuring that women are always part of the public dialogue, conducted an analysis of announced commencement speakers in the top 50 colleges and universities in the U.S. in 2019. GenderAvenger found that it was a "shockingly balanced group" made up of 33 men and 33 women, including 12 women of color.[99] (Some schools have more than one speaker.) Good news, right? Sure, but there's more to it. "A look at the same top 50 universities used to evaluate commencement speakers revealed that just 8 out of 50 have women presidents or chancellors—that's only 16%, which is far lower than the average," according to GenderAvenger. "Featuring women on commencement stages is important, but we need to be sure they are not being used to mask deeper gender imbalance throughout the system." Well said, GenderAvenger.

Lead with Your Values

These are just some of the strategies you can employ to align your organization's hiring policies with your commitment to dignity, diversity, and inclusion. More will occur to you as you continue to develop as a Dignity Mindset-driven leader and as you communicate your priorities to your human resources department, your hiring/interviewing team, and the recruiters with whom you choose to work.

Whenever you're making any kind of choices about recruiting, interviewing, and hiring, keep bringing yourself back to the commitment you've made for yourself and your organization to make every recruitment strategy and every hire align with your core values of dignity, diversity, and inclusion. Imagine how much change you can bring about in your organization when you make dignity your top priority.

Take Trust to the Next Level

"The first job of a leader ... is to inspire trust. It's to bring out the best in people by entrusting them with meaningful stewardships, and to create an environment in which high-trust interaction inspires creativity and possibility."

— The late Stephen R. Covey, business consultant and author of
The Speed of Trust: The One Thing that Changes Everything

Trust is a cornerstone of a Dignity Mindset. Leaders who recognize the importance of trust, who seek to foster it in themselves and their organizations, and who honor it as a core value earn the loyalty of their employees and the respect of their industries.

In an organization, trust shows up in many ways, including transparency, fairness, and power sharing. When leaders demonstrate trustworthiness themselves and expect it from everyone in their organization, many of the roadblocks that stand in the way of dignity, inclusion, and self-actualization begin to fall away. In a high-trust environment, employees—especially those who have experienced prejudice, bias, and marginalization— start to consider the possibility of letting their guard down. When trust makes room for unguarded self-expression and a feeling of safety, employees are better able to set aside their bias-based anxieties and focus instead on performing at their highest possible levels. High-trust environments provide the safe, supportive atmosphere in which employees can fulfill their fundamental need to self-actualize and realize their full creative and business potential.

What exactly is trust? To start with, it's a belief in the character, reliability, or strength of another person. It is the foundation of all human connections and interactions, both at work and in life. Stephen R. Covey, the author of many game-changing books (Including *The Speed of Trust*), has contributed so much in-depth work to our understanding of trust. He describes trust as the one thing that, if developed and leveraged, "has the potential to create unparalleled success and prosperity in every dimension of life."[100]

One of my favorite definitions of trust comes from an executive education student who participated in a workshop I led: "Trust is *my* ability to predict how *you* will behave in the future with something that *I* care about." Well said!

Depending on the situation, trust can include some other elements, too. For example, you can count on people you trust to:

+ Deliver *what* they promise, *when* they promise it
+ Have your back in any situation
+ Behave with integrity even when nobody else is looking
+ Stand up for you, whether or not you're not in the room
+ Give you a head's up if you're going in the wrong direction
+ Coach you to improvement
+ Celebrate your success and be present with you when you fail
+ Let you know if things are being said about you or your work behind your back
+ Offer constructive feedback *in private* with thoughtfulness and care
+ Be transparent, honest, and truthful

Whom Do You Trust?

Here's an exercise I do in some of my workshops to help people gain perspective on trust. I ask them the following three questions:

1. Thinking of yourself, privately make a list of the people in your organization that you trust.
2. Next, make a list of the people in your organization who would put *your* name on *their* list of people that they trust.

3. Finally, write down the names of the people you trust who hold positions of power and influence in your organization.

This exercise usually creates stunned silence, as people realize how elusive trust is. I see in participants' eyes how disappointed they are to have such short lists. And, not surprisingly, based on conversations I have with participants afterward, trust lists are briefer for women than men, and briefest of all for women of color. Too many people—especially women and people of color—are working in a low-trust environment.

Trust Helps Your Business

Aiming to take trust to the next level with the goal of building a high-trust, dignity-driven atmosphere isn't just the right thing to do for your employees. Raising trust is also in your organization's best interest. Proof of that comes from many sources, including Great Place to Work, a global people analytics and consulting firm that helps companies produce better business results by focusing on workplace culture. In addition to compiling lists of Best Companies to Work For, the firm helps organizations build a high-trust, high-performance culture.[101]

For more than 30 years, Great Place to Work has studied high-trust workplace cultures and has collected data on their performance. The data makes a compelling argument in favor of focusing on high trust as a top priority for organizational success. For example, the company's research has found the following:[102]

- High-trust organizations are rewarded with impressive stock market performance. Among publicly traded companies on the 100 Best Companies to Work For list, stock market returns are three times greater than market average.
- High trust influences employee turnover rates. "Across industries, we've found a high-trust culture means 50% lower voluntary turnover—and huge cost savings,"

Great Place to Work reports. "At the 100 Best Companies to Work For, an average of 87% of all employees say they 'want to work here for a long time.'"

+ In addition, high-trust organizations experience higher staff productivity, more engaged workers, more innovation, and happier customers.

What does a high-trust culture look like in a workplace? Here's how Great Place to Work describes it: "It's a workplace where employees believe leaders are credible (competent, communicative, honest), they are treated with respect as people and professionals, and the workplace is fundamentally fair for everyone. When workplaces do all these things well, employees feel empowered and the business flourishes."

The Current State of Trust

Despite the obvious benefits of trustworthiness in corporate America, the current state of trust leaves much to be desired. According to a global survey of professionals in eight countries conducted by Ernst & Young in 2016, fewer than half of global respondents have a "great deal of trust" in their current employers, bosses, or colleagues. Trust levels are even lower among women, who reported that they were more likely than men to look for another job or make less effort at work because of low trust.[103] In addition, compared with men, women were more likely to consider workplace diversity and pay and promotion opportunities as "very important" factors in trusting their employers.

According to EY, the top five factors leading to respondents' lack of trust in their employers were:

+ unfair employee compensation
+ unequal opportunity for pay and promotion
+ lack of leadership
+ high employee turnover
+ a work environment not conducive to collaboration.

When we consider women of color, the EY survey only reinforces that trust is even lower among them, which is no surprise considering that they are the most underrepresented group in corporate America,[104] have an even greater gender pay gap than white women,[105] and are more likely than white women to experience sexual harassment at work.[106] The trust gap in organizations can be attributed in large part to the biases (both unconscious and conscious) that exist in the current core power structure, which continues to be populated primarily by straight white men. These biases have allowed powerful leaders to inflict all kinds of damage on women, people of color, and other marginalized populations, from micro-aggressions to job loss, sexual harassment, and rape. One could argue that with #MeToo, Time's Up, and other movements, industries and their leaders are being held accountable in ways that had not happened in the past. However, it takes time, effort, and paradigm shifts—such as a serious buy-in to and demonstration of the Dignity Mindset in action—to build trust.

As we talk about trust, it's important to recognize that we must redefine it to reflect the needs of all people, not just the white male power structure. We must hold trust to a stronger standard, one that not only includes conventional thinking (like Covey's) but an absolute commitment to inclusion and diversity. A leader's trustworthiness must extend to every person in an organization, not just the straight white men on the executive team. Just as everyone has the same worth and the same fundamental human needs as everyone else, everyone has the same need for—and right to—a high-trust work environment. This next-level trust is a fundamental and essential duty of the dignity-driven leader.

Start Building Trust Now

The idea of constructing a high-trust environment within your organization may feel overwhelming. Although it's true that you can't build trust overnight—especially in an organization that has fallen short on trustworthiness in the past—you can take some important steps to start turning that around.

Begin with the simple act of announcing that you are setting the intention of becoming more trustworthy yourself, and of raising trust levels in every part of your organization. When you let others know that you are intentionally working to elevate trust, you put them on notice that you will be changing your words and behaviors, and you expect them to do so also. Share the dignity-driven thought processes behind your intention of taking trust to the next level, making sure to highlight the potential advantages to your employees and your organization. When people understand all the positive results that can occur when trust levels go up, they're likely to feel motivated to join you in your commitment to this important priority.

Once you've made your intention and commitment public, remember that even the smallest actions—often the most powerful ones—can begin to bring about changes. People *want* to trust their leaders and the organizations for which they work. They don't like being in a low-trust environment. However, although words are a good way to start, your promises must be followed by actions, including the ones that follow.

Offer Greater Transparency About Pay

Being open about how much the people in your organization earn is one of the best ways to walk the talk on trust. Employees can't work together at their highest levels in an open, trusting way when they worry that the colleagues sitting next to them are receiving higher pay for the same level of work. Unfortunately, pay transparency remains uncommon, according to the 2019 Compensation Programs & Practices Survey conducted by WorldatWork, an association of total rewards professionals.[107] The findings, compared with earlier surveys going back to 2010, showed that pay-related information was shared by only 47% of employers. They also found that more employers are now sharing less information about individual salaries than in 2010.

"The results point to the need for much more transparency about how compensations programs work, especially when we see continued concerns about miscommunication, wage gaps, and pay inequities," says Scott Cawood, President and CEO of WorldatWork. "This isn't the time to retreat into sharing less information with your employees which, in fact, ...

could backfire. People want to know how to succeed in organizations and that starts with understanding how compensation programs are designed and administered."

In recent years, breaking with an unwritten cultural law in just about every work environment, women have begun to ask each other to share their compensation, so as a collective there is a sense of the severity of the gap among themselves. This can be very uncomfortable for some women, and they have found that offering a range in which their pay sits as a way to contribute to the effort. It's important not to blame women colleagues who may ask for this transparency, because the blame lies with the fact that there's an unfair gender pay gap.

Of course, in order to be transparent about pay you have to take pay gaps seriously and eliminate any gaps related to gender, race, or other factors. (Read about how Marc Benioff, chairman and co-CEO at Salesforce, did this in Tool #1: Be a Dignity-Driven Leader.) Right now, the gender pay gap is 80%[108] for women overall (meaning that on average, women earn 80 cents for every dollar men earn), 61% for black women, and 53% percent for Latinx women.[109] The gender pay gap affects women of every age group, at every education level, in every type of job, in every demographic, and in every state in the country. Although it has improved over the past 40 years (it was 60 percent in 1980), improvement has stagnated over the past two decades, according to a 2018 report[110] issued by the American Association of University Women (AAUW).

Eliminating pay gaps in your organization and being transparent about what everyone makes goes a long way toward building trust. Transparency can't end with pay; trust also grows when organizations offer greater transparency about hiring, promotion, and performance, including being open about gender and race.

Own Your Mistakes

Another crucial way to build trust is to own your mistakes. If you're not in the habit of taking full responsibility for your errors and slip-ups, it's time to start. There really are few behaviors more powerful and more trust-building than acknowledging that you've done something wrong, offering a full apology—not that weak "I'm sorry *if* you were offended" non-apology—and making a commitment to change your behavior in the future. (For step by-step advice on how to make an apology, see Tool #3: Communicate with Dignity By Mastering Seven Consequential Conversations.) We all make mistakes; owning them shows others that you have a true commitment to behaving in alignment with your core values and holding yourself accountable when you don't.

Open Up Decision-Making

If the majority of important decisions in your organization are made by a room full of predominantly straight white men, it's time to change that. Opening up decision-making processes to include a diverse group of people with *real power* will help build trust, because it demonstrates in a very public way that you trust the people in the group to handle important responsibilities, such as choosing a candidate for an important role. If you do open up your decision-making processes, make sure you keep your commitment to transparency *for the entire process*. If you appoint a diverse committee to spearhead a selection process, for example, you must stay committed to the group from beginning to end. You can't step back and let them do their work and then swoop in and take over at the last minute. I've seen this happen with unfortunate frequency—a committee works diligently and then at the end discovers that their recommendations have been ignored and someone else has been selected without their knowledge. What a slap in the face, and what a way to poison trust. Not only do the people on the committee feel that they've wasted their time, but they are angered that they've been used in a pretense of openness that leaves them out of the information loop. It's the reason Cindy Robbins, the chief personnel officer at Salesforce, told Benioff he couldn't go halfway with his pay gap investigation.

Adding diversity to decision-making has the potential to benefit your organization as well as your employees. Trust and integrity are inextricably linked. Research has shown that diversity on corporate boards is an effective way to reduce risk. According to Catalyst, for example, gender-diverse boards have fewer instances of controversial business practices such as fraud, corruption, bribery, and shareholder battles compared with homogenous boards.[111] They are also associated with fewer financial reporting mistakes and better collection and transparent disclosure of stock price information.

Homogenous groups tend to engage more often in groupthink than diverse groups. A board full of straight white men with nearly identical backgrounds are more likely to hold similar viewpoints and have similar perspectives than a diverse board. It's easy to engage in groupthink when you're surrounded by people who look and live a lot like you. And it's harder to question each other's opinions and decisions without feeling that you're letting the group down or worrying that you may face retaliation down the road.

Understand That Trust is Even Harder for Women of Color

As we've discussed, women are less likely than men to trust their employers. But the trust gap is even wider for women of color. As a dignity-driven leader who believes that everyone in your organization has the same worth and the same fundamental human needs as everyone else, it's important for you to understand what lies behind the trust gap among women of color.

Earlier in this book we examined how hegemonic male power belief systems impact women at every point of their lives and are reinforced by cinema, video gaming, social media, education, and various other cultural factors. These forces affect all women, but they have an even greater detrimental impact on women of color. For these reasons, and because of other factors that go beyond the scope of this book, women of color in the workplace can find it very challenging to trust their leaders and their organization. So many roadblocks stand between them and the satisfactory achievement of their fundamental human needs.

Workforce data and my own experience working with many high-performing and high-potential women of color suggest that most of them literally don't believe that *anyone* in the organization has their back, or that there is *anyone* in the core power structure that they can fully trust. Remember the "whom do you trust" exercise I mentioned earlier? There's often *nobody* on their lists. Imagine how that feels. Try to envision how much more complex the day is for a woman of color who is gifted, ambitious, and unsure of how any of her co-workers will respond to things she cares about. Go back to the definition of trust shared with me by one of my students: "Trust is *my* ability to predict how *you* will behave in the future with something that *I* care about." Too many women of color don't have the ability to predict how others in their organization will behave about things they care about. Contrast this low-trust wariness with the high-trust informal networks of the straight white males, who can easily predict how others will behave in relation to the things they care about. What a stark difference.

Imagine the loneliness, emotional isolation, and endless second- and third-guessing of high-performing, high-potential women of color. So often in their lives they have been *the only*. Every day they face micro-aggressions ("Honey, can you get me a cup of coffee?" or "You just need to prove yourself for another year or so.") and insulting comments ("Why would you want to push for the top job? You'll open yourself up to so much scrutiny—are you sure you can handle that?"), not to mention outright prejudice and harassment.

Despite all this, women of color rise up from the lack of respect, the degradations, and the absence of advocacy to run teams, divisions, lines of business, and entire organizations (though not nearly enough of them) with a strength of character, clarity of purpose, and personal integrity that has been tested and retested so many times that it's nearly impossible to knock them over. They show a core of strength that often sets them apart—if only there were more people willing to open their eyes to see it. Oprah Winfrey, former PepsiCo CEO Indra Nooyi, Sofia Vergara (the highest paid[112] TV actress in 2018), Patsy Takemoto Mink (the first woman of color in Congress and an original architect of Title IX)—there are so many amazing examples of women of color with tremendous grit, guts, courage, smarts, and ambition.

Just think about how your organization could benefit if it could get out of its own way and open pathways to allow remarkable women like these to reach their greatest potential, rather than undercutting them every single day through bias and lack of trust.

Here's another thing to keep in mind when considering hiring and promoting women of color: They have credentials and ambition and stand ready to lead. According to a report[113] by the Center for Talent Innovation, "black women are more likely than their white female counterparts to understand the benefits of a powerful position and are more likely to strive for the top jobs." The report also found that black women are "more likely to perceive a powerful position as the means to achieving their professional goals and are confident that they can succeed in the role." In addition, the study found the following[114]:

- Black women are more likely than white women to aspire to a powerful position with a prestigious title (22% vs. 8%).
- 44% of black women feel stalled in their careers (as compared to 30% of white women).
- Black women without power are more likely than white women without power (26% vs. 14%) to perceive that an executive role will allow them to flourish.

As you can see, there is so much evidence that black women and other women of color are ready to lead. And yet, only 1 in 5 senior leaders is a woman, 1 in 25 is a woman of color.

By taking trust to the next level in your organization, you'll create the space these brilliant women need to shine.

Take Micro-aggressions Seriously

Let's look again at the table we provided in the confidence section of Tool #2: Create an Inclusion Institute. In that table, we focused on the lasting impact micro-aggressions have on women's confidence. But as we consider ways to take trust to the next level, it's important to recognize that micro-aggressions also impact an organization's ability to demonstrate trustworthiness and to attract and retain women of all colors.

In light of our discussion about trust, I'll add three more micro-aggressions to the ones I mentioned in that table: Hiding pay gap numbers, failing to address biased words or actions in performance reviews, and failing to communicate rationale for promotions. Each of these denies the fundamental need for esteem, belonging, and self-actualization.

As you set goals to educate your employees about the damage micro-aggressions can cause to people and your organization, remember that it's not enough for leaders to say "We won't tolerate micro-aggressions." You have to walk the talk. You can't have a town hall about reducing micro-aggressions and then go back to your office and set up a golf date with Mike and Bill that excludes Janelle and Zoe.

It's easy to ignore micro-aggressions—after all, they're small, right? Wrong. Micro-aggressions add up in a most nefarious way, breaking down the trust you are working hard to build up. In extreme cases they can lead to litigation and public relations disasters; more often, they result in poor team performance, toxicity in a team's climate, decreased engagement among employees, less agility, loss of talented team members, and a poor showing on Best Places to Work lists.

Trust Makes Dignity Possible

When you take trust to the next level with yourself and your organization, you make so many amazing things possible. You create a setting in which people can feel empowered, rather than beaten down. You make it possible for them to let down their guard and focus on performing at their very highest levels. And you remove the roadblocks that hold so many women—particularly women of color—from unleashing their potential.

Don't let that happen any longer. You are in a unique position to facilitate women's success for themselves, for your organization, and for the world. As Indra Nooyi has been quoted as saying, "Please help others rise. Greatness comes not from a position, but from helping build the future. We have an obligation to pull others up."

DIGNITY MINDSET TOOL #6

Open Up Your Networks

"Networking has been cited as the number one unwritten rule of success in business. <u>Who</u> you know really impacts <u>what</u> you know."

— Sallie Krawcheck, CEO and co-founder of Ellevest, a digital financial advisor for women and author of the book *Own It: The Power of Women at Work*

Personal networks are vital currency for all of us. Networks have the potential to provide information, access, power, and influence. A network built up over years or decades provides valuable business and social capital as well as access to a web of relationships. Strong networks are often *the* key difference when the stakes are high: One good connection can turn a job search into a job offer, can offer entrée to a board placement, or can provide the net that catches you when you fall.

In business, having a robust network offers a range of advantages. "The research on power and influence shows that people who are well networked are three times more influential than people who aren't," says Terry R. Bacon, a leadership researcher and author of the book *The Elements of Power: Lessons on Leadership and Influence.*[115] When you're facing a business challenge, it's tremendously helpful to have the opportunity to reach out to someone you know for assistance, advice, or reassurance. In addition, networks are a crucial component in talent acquisition: According to a LinkedIn survey, as many as 85% of jobs are filled via some type of networking.[116]

The problem with networks is that unless people are quite intentional about making them inclusive, they tend to resemble heavy-walled silos, because we tend to build networks with people who are just like us. Insular networks limit connections between groups and only reinforce the heavy walls that prop up bias and exclusion in organizations. If you're a straight white male in the core power structure, your network is probably made up mostly of straight white males who also occupy that power structure. Because of the homogeneity of informal networks, members of marginalized groups who are locked out of core power networks have much to lose.

Ask any professional woman if she's ever experienced being shut out of the boys' club at work, and she's very likely to say yes. Too many workplaces are closed systems, or closed social shops, where hegemonic masculinity rules. In these environments, employees are divided into insiders and outsiders where a one up/one down paradigm sets the tone.

Of course, people in power may maintain exclusivity within their networks as a way to reinforce and protect the power of their own race or gender—they like the idea of working within a closed shop. (Augusta National Golf Club, one of the most famous golf clubs in the world, didn't admit African Americans as members until 1990 and only began admitting women in 2012. Now that's a closed shop.) But networks can also remain closed for less harmful reasons.

The onus of opening up these insular network silos must rest not on marginalized groups, but on the straight white men who inhabit the core power structure. As a leader who is committed to dignity and diversity, you can immediately start taking steps to make your organization's networks more useful to a greater number of people by opening them up. In this section, we'll explore some of the many ways to do this. By applying a Dignity Mindset to informal and formal networks, you pave the way to increase diversity while sparking innovation and organizational success.

Speaking Up About Networks

Progressive leaders who approach business with a Dignity Mindset recognize the value of overhauling out-of-date networks. The first and easiest thing they can do is to speak up to their senior leaders—not by calling out but by calling in—to point out the absence of women, people of color, and members of the LGBTQ community in lunchrooms, at golf outings, and wherever the members of a traditionally male core power structure gather. Dignity-driven leaders communicate a clear, unequivocal message of inclusion to straight white male executives that it's time to diversify their networks—proactively—and for many, this requires developing skills to do so.

This tactic doesn't have to cost a thing, and it doesn't have to take a lot of time. You can accomplish so much simply by putting responsibility where it belongs and demonstrating strong leadership to the men in the core power network. Consider the path taken by JPMorgan Chase & Co., which recently launched what it refers to as its "30-5-1 Campaign." According to the company, the campaign's message and strategy are simple: Spending a total of just 36 minutes a week can help advance women in the company. Here's how that 36 minutes breaks down:

- Spend **30 minutes a week** having coffee with a talented up-and-coming woman.
- Spend **5 minutes a week** congratulating a female colleague on a win or success.
- Spend **1 minute a week** talking up the woman who had that win to other colleagues around the firm.[117]

The campaign, sponsored by the company's Women on the Move initiative, was created to support women's growth and development. "By encouraging a culture of open dialogue and interaction across all levels and business groups, Women on the Move aims to see an increase in the number of women in senior management positions at the firm," the company says. The link between open networks and gender equity at the top are irrefutable.

Shifting the Network Onus

Up to now, the burden for closing the distance that comes with being "the other" in an organization has rested with individuals who are left out. It's time to flip that around and shift the responsibility to the straight white men in the core power structure. Outsiders inside the organization already face enough challenges at work.

When men share the access they already have—including access to people in power through formal and informal networks—they can finally relieve women, people of color, and LGBTQ individuals from having to take on this daunting task themselves. They also help remove the social parallelism that often exists in corporate networks today.

What do I mean by social parallelism? In many but not all organizations, there's the typical core power structure, and parallel networks of special interest networks (also known as employee resource groups or affinity groups) made up of everyone else. Special interest networks for diversity and inclusion are created for good reasons: to facilitate supportive connections among professionals who often feel alone in the typical meeting on a typical day. They're a way for marginalized individuals to reduce feelings of isolation that comes with otherhood and to ensure that the vital information to which they might not otherwise have access is shared across the group. This can be a welcome relief for people who spend so much of their days being outsiders.

Even though these kinds of networks exist for good reason, the downside is that continued separation of networks—like so many separate bubbles—fails to provide outsiders with access to power. Leaders driven by the values of a Dignity Mindset interrupt parallel networking by ensuring affiliation and relationship development as opportunities for everyone.

Opening up networks does so much more than simply benefiting those on the outside. When straight white men bring others into their networks, they discover a full range of new ideas about how to approach business challenges and opportunities.

Perhaps you work at a drug company, where brilliant new product development is performed by people with extraordinary credentials working in the trenches. These employees—which typically include many more women and people of color than the executive team—make the company successful through their efforts to get a new drug developed and approved. But when it comes time to showcase important new work to the CEO, do your managers invite the people who are actually doing the work to present their updates to top management? Or do the managers use those opportunities to boost their own exposure to the CEO? Open up the network and spotlight the people who are driving the company's success. Dignity-driven leaders insist that the talent on the ground present updates on their own work at high-level meetings, even if it means upsetting a longstanding gentlemen's agreement with a male manager. If they don't, the downstream impact is quite predictable: The esteem needs of key talent are violated. After a while they accept those ongoing headhunter calls, and one day they're gone. Then the CEO is back to square one, wondering: "Why can't we retain women here?"

ONA: Making the Invisible Visible

A fantastic tool known as organizational network analysis (ONA) can provide insights into how inclusivity is managed in your company. This essential management tool—which is like taking an X-ray of what's happening underneath the surface of your company—helps leaders understand how employees are actually getting work done and who is doing it. It also shines a light on natural networks in practice: who's in the center of it all, who's the go-to for various issues, who's a point of logjam, and who could be contributing more but is being shut out.

ONA management tools can provide insights into the makeup of your informal networks and highlight opportunities to increase diversity by "making the invisible visible," as a Deloitte report so aptly puts it.[118] ONAs are developed by collecting data about employee interactions using surveys, and by examining emails, electronic meeting invitations, and other communications that shine a light into the engine of the work. ONA data maps are most often used to inform reorganizations, but when those maps aren't tapped to examine inclusion, it's truly a lost opportunity.

Increasing inclusion in both formal and informal networks helps eliminate a barrier that results from unfamiliarity. Consciously or not, people tend to hire, promote, and work with people in their network. This is because they know and trust each other—recall in Tool #5: Take Trust to the Next Level, that we defined trust as "my ability to predict how you will behave in the future about things I care about." And of course I really care about how you make me look when I promote you. Informal familiarity leads to relationships, and relationships lead to inclusion. Having more open networks makes it easier to move from "I don't know you well enough" to "I want to promote you to this new role." The more women in your network, the more likely you are to create a healthy web of interdependent, respectful relationships across gender.

A variety of vendors offer ONA tools. Leaders can work with their human resources director to choose a vendor and platform that best suit an organization's needs and budget. ONA is such a powerful tool that it's surprising more organizations don't use it to diversify homogenous closed shops. We know how beneficial open networks can be for individuals and businesses. ONA can deliver significant impact for retention efforts of not only women, but members of the LGBTQ community, people of color, and others who feel they are working on an unseen stage.

Look Around

Some closed networks are so obvious you don't need management tools and data analysis to identify them. You really just have to open your eyes to see them. That's what happened with a wonderful, seasoned CEO whom I admire because of his highly developed Dignity Mindset. He recently shared with me that he had noticed clear gender segregation in his organization's lunchroom. He pointed it out to the men on his executive team and suggested they disperse among the other employees at lunch with a goal of building new relationships. He told them he never again wanted to come to lunch and see all the senior executive white men sitting only with each other. They took his advice, and he said it was a small but important step in opening up the connections between different groups of people in his company.

This CEO did something about the lopsided nature of the corporate playing field in the lunchroom and dealt with it instead of denying it. He definitely put his Dignity Mindset values into practice. A leader cannot espouse diversity while keeping silent about the existence of obvious marginalization and closed networks within an organization's ranks.

While ONA is a very powerful tool to see the inner workings of people and teams, there are other ways progressive organizations are changing up their tactics to boost inclusive networking. A platform known as Lunch

Roulette (https://lunchroulette.us) uses automation to randomly pair people within an organization for lunch. The founders of Lunch Roulette created the platform because they "believe this process can break down silos, improve communication, and improve workplace satisfaction."[119] Once they sign up, employees are paired twice a month (or at an interval of your choosing) for lunch with someone new. A platform like this is helpful for organizations that need to do a better job of facilitating networking of employees at all levels.

Here's another great example of a leader opening networks by observing his workplace in a thoughtful, value-driven way. In an article for *Medium*, Australian entrepreneur Alan Downie wrote about some of the things he noticed when his team moved from a co-working space to its first office. Downie, founder of Splitrock Studio, a startup collective, recalls that a ping pong table was one of the group's first purchases.

Although players had fun, Downie began to notice that the ping pong table became a device that separated the team into groups: super intense players, players, and non-players. He saw how this "in" or "out" of the ping pong club culture began to have a negative impact on relationships, informal connecting, and the group's climate in general. The ping pong table is a central element in all kinds of organizations, especially in Silicon Valley and the bro culture there.

"I decided to gift the table to one of the staff to take home, and it was the best thing we ever did," Downie wrote. "We replaced it with a lunch table, some nice chairs, and a collection of board games. Instead of having a team coming together to beat each other at table tennis (and thereby excluding those who didn't play), we had a team sitting down to enjoy a meal or a game of cards together."[120]

Downie's decision makes so much sense. He looked around, saw something that was creating exclusion, and made a change that aligned with his Dignity Mindset. The table had become a dividing line "between those who do and those who don't." After the table was taken away, the room went from an exclusive space to an inclusive space. Downie recognizes that other leaders may have chosen to keep the ping pong table because of the argument that anyone could choose to play—or not. "It's true, but young active dudes play far more often and far more competitively. Anyone who isn't a young active dude is far less likely to enjoy that environment." Let's face it: That kind of competitive, high-testosterone play is a major turn-off for a lot of people—including (but not only) a lot of women. That literal roar of competition isn't interesting to, or welcomed by, lots of people at work, and it reinforces some of the informal networks that can marginalize certain team members. Downie's article is a great read for younger executives who are ready to move beyond "it's all about me" and instead seek to make business decisions that align with the values of inclusivity and dignity.

Extend Your Own Network

You can begin to open up your own personal and business networks by taking advantage of opportunities to meet, connect with, and stay in touch with a more diverse group of people. Engaging with people who are just like you is like sinking into a warm bath; instead, challenge yourself to jump into a bracing pool of cool water occasionally by spending time with people with whom you may at first glance think you have little in common. For many who have made the effort, the result has been highly worthwhile.

One of the biggest hindrances to breaking through informal social barriers is not quite knowing how to break the ice. Putting yourself in the same room with people isn't enough; you have to be intentional about making a connection and starting to build a new relationship.

You may not necessarily find it easy at first to talk with people who are other than you. That's okay. But it shouldn't stop you from learning how to do this—it's a skill you can learn. Start by figuring out what questions to ask—and not to ask. Recently Terri Nimmons, CEO of Stone Lake Leadership Group, surveyed a group of African American women about what they like (and don't like) to be asked about. Here's what they said:

DO Ask Me About:

- ◆ My interests as a person
- ◆ My projects at work
- ◆ One thing you could do to remove any barriers blocking me from my full potential

- My kids and any passions they may have, if you're talking about your kids

DO NOT Ask Me About:

- What school I went to
- What town I live in (and other socioeconomic questions)
- Politics
- Professional sports
- My hair
- Race

If talking with people with whom you share little in common poses a challenge, work with your human resources manager or a corporate coach to come up with lists like these for people of backgrounds that differ from yours. Doing some homework on this issue will help you push past the reluctance you may have about taking the lead in connecting with people different from yourself.

Become a Mentor

Another wonderful way to expand your connections with people of different backgrounds is to take on a mentorship role. All leaders are mentors, to some extent, but entering into a formal mentor relationship with individuals who have experienced bias has the potential to teach you so much about people outside your usual network. Most mentors find that they get as much out of a mentorship relationship as the mentee—if not more.

Part of your job as a mentor is to transfer knowledge, share your experiences, and support mentees as they learn new skills. As a mentor who approaches each day with a Dignity Mindset, you're in a unique position to help your mentees navigate bias, meet their fundamental needs, and move toward self-actualization. You can serve as their guide and their champion. (You may also consider being a sponsor, which is different from a mentor.

A mentor is more of an advisor; a sponsor tends to take a more active role in facilitating career opportunities and preparing an individual for promotion.)

Mentors can learn so much from mentees who have experienced bias and marginalization. Nothing drives home the reality of bias more effectively than hearing stories from people who have experienced it. Ask mentees about how bias and hegemonic masculinity have shown up in their lives, and don't flinch when they share their stories. It's important for all leaders to have exposure to the reality of bias.

For tips on how to design an effective mentorship program, refer back to Tool #2: Create an Inclusion Institute.

Make a Conscious, Dignity-Based Choice

It's fair to say that many straight white men don't set out in a highly conscious way to exclude; rather they find themselves in closed clubs simply as a result doing what comes naturally to them and associating with other people in their circles who are just like them. It's not an indictment; it's human nature. We all do it. But because membership in these exclusive networks has a potentially huge impact on career mobility, wages, and business success, all leaders choosing to adopt a Dignity Mindset must also commit to intentionally opening and diversifying their networks.

A Dignity Mindset helps you to be proactive in looking at who's on the inside and who's on the outside. Remember, outsiders by definition are not having their essential need for belonging met, and this creates low engagement and satisfaction and low trust. By opening up your network and creating more open connections among your employees, you exponentially increase opportunities for inclusion, retention, optimization of key talent, and organizational success.

Measure Progress Through Accountability

"Women have immense talents that society does not leverage. And we are impoverished by not having access to that talent."

— Christine Lagarde, Managing Director and
Chairwoman of the International Monetary Fund

Throughout this book we've looked at the ways in which biased male hegemonic belief systems influence the U.S. workforce, and some of the steps that enlightened leaders who have adopted a Dignity Mindset can take to start to reframe those beliefs. So far, we've looked at six important tools that can guide you as you create more diverse, inclusive teams in your organization. These tools offer you a wealth of specific strategies and tactics, as well as inspiration to direct you as you design your own dignity-based goals.

Our seventh and last tool is actually one of the most important, because it helps ensure follow-through on all of the others. In this last section, we examine ways in which to measure progress through accountability.

Measurement matters because, as business guru Peter Drucker is believed to have said, "What gets measured gets managed." How true that is. Measurement involves an objective gathering of data that allows us to compare results with goals, and to determine whether business processes are delivering value. Only when we track outcomes do we discover the effectiveness of our actions and choices.

When measurement shows shortfalls, organizations can go back and manage processes in a different way to better align them with the outcomes they seek. Ultimately, measuring is the key to change, growth, and progress. It also necessitates transparency, which is crucial to change.

In the pages that follow, we'll look at some of the ways in which measurement and transparency can make a difference for women, women of color, and other groups that are subject to bias. The recommended approaches, tools, and technologies will come in handy as you align your company with the values and practices of a Dignity Mindset.

Regulating Equity

When it comes to gender equity, measurement and accountability must begin at the global level. Governments have played a huge role in moving women forward in countries all over the world: for example, in Rwanda, Iceland, and in the United States with Title IX. But now it's time to join countries like France and Germany in making laws that require public companies to meet specific equity requirements, to report their progress in an open way, and to be held accountable when they fall short. And when governments fail to require equity, organizations must step up and take responsibility for it themselves.

We have so much work to do in this regard. In the United States, the gender pay gap has stalled over the past couple decades; women overall earn an average of only about 80 cents for every dollar a man earns, black women earn 61 cents for every dollar a man makes, and Latinx women receive 53 cents for a man's dollar.[121] Likewise, female representation on corporate boards remains stuck at only around 21%.[122] (And as we've discussed, these gaps are even greater for women of color.) Management of these inequities must begin at the top, with a push from government and a requirement for measurement and public reporting.

When governments involve themselves in equity requirements, change happens— proof that what gets measured gets managed. And often what gets managed gets changed. According to Catalyst, research has shown that countries "with specific targets, quotas, and penalties for not meeting regulations—including Norway, Iceland, Finland, and Sweden—had nearly double the average percentage of women on boards (about 34%) than countries without those regulations (about 18%)."[123] Countries that regulate equity are choosing to live with contemporary values of equality, rather than clinging to belief systems created thousands of years ago.

Choosing Female Leaders

Electing more women, and more women of color, to representative roles in government also helps drive the development of laws that require measurement and reporting on issues affecting women, especially in cultures like the U.S. where gender imbalance is so significant. The U.S. has made *some* progress lately—much was made of the increase in number of women elected 2018, leading to a record number of women in Congress. But we still have a long way to go, as we see when we step back and measure our progress with a global perspective.

Despite 2018's record-breaking gains in Congress, the U.S. still lags behind much of the world when it comes to female representation, ranking at a dismally low #75 in a list compiled by the Inter-Parliamentary Union.[124] The U.S. has much to learn from societies that rank highest on that list, including #1 Rwanda (61% female representation) as well as Cuba and Bolivia (53%), Mexico (48%), Grenada (47%), Namibia, Sweden, Nicaragua, and Costa Rica (46%), and South Africa (43%). Go down, down, down the list and you'll find the U.S. with 23.5%.

As Gates Foundation co-founder Melinda Gates says, "It's a better time in the world to be a woman than it has ever been—yet it's not getting better fast enough."[125] That certainly is true in the U.S.

Measuring the Impact of Equal Pay

What would happen if we could eliminate the 80% gender pay gap in the U.S. and compensate women as well as men? The payoff would be amazing, considering that the gender pay gap causes women to lose out on more than $500 billion in earnings each year.[126] To start with, almost 60% of women would earn more if they were paid the same as men with equivalent levels of education and work hours.[127] Eliminating the gender pay gap would also pull many women out of poverty, cutting the poverty rate in half for working women. And as women's lives improved, so too would the lives of some 2.5 million children who depend on the support of working mothers, according to a 2018 report from the American Association of University Women (AAUW).[128]

"If women in the United States received equal pay with comparable men, poverty for working women would be reduced by half and the U.S. economy would have added $482 billion (equivalent to 2.8 percent of 2014 GDP) to its economy," according to the Institute for Women's Policy Research.[129]

Erasing the pay gap would also allow women to pay off billions in dollars of student debt, because lower salaries make it harder for them to repay college loans. (Incidentally, two-thirds of student debt is owed by women).[130] In addition, pay equity would impact women's retirement: Because Social Security payments and pensions are based on income, the over-65 retirement income pay gap is currently a shockingly low 52 percent for white women compared to white men, and even lower for non-white women. In fact, eliminating the gap would help *everyone* finance their retirement by significantly increasing Social Security funding. "If we close the pay gap and increase earnings for women, then we can close Social Security savings shortfall by $4.7 trillion, or 35%," according to Katica Roy, CEO and founder of Pipeline.[131] "Closing the gender pay gap moves us toward the solvency of Social Security, benefiting all working Americans and ensuring everyone paying into Social Security actually receives their benefits."

Recognizing the Impact of Disclosure

An effective way to start eliminating the gender pay gap is to institute government-mandated reporting of gender pay discrepancies. When researchers Morten Bennedsen, Elena Simintzi, Margarita Tsoutsoura, and Daniel Wolfenzon conducted the first empirical study on the impact of mandatory wage transparency, they found that disclosing disparities in gender pay does in fact narrow the gender wage gap, according to their *Harvard Business Review* article about the study.[132] Mandatory disclosure also leads to more female hires, more female promotions to senior positions, and less money spent overall on wages due to the slowing down of the growth of male wages.

"Our research suggests that governments' efforts to address these disparities through transparency can be effective—and beneficial to firms as well as to their female employees," the researchers wrote.

Efforts to close gender pay gaps often fail. One reason for this is money; bringing women's salaries into line with men's pay may require some initial investment, as Salesforce CEO Marc Benioff learned when he spent $10.3 million[133] (as of this writing) to close pay gaps in his organization. However, over the long term, they can produce significant benefit for all stakeholders, especially when factoring in the savings that result when high-performing women stay in their jobs rather than moving around in hopes of finding a dignity-driven organization that operates with transparency, trust, and fairness.

Another reason for failure is that evening up pay rates requires an ongoing commitment, rather than a one-and-done approach. "Companies serious about pay initiatives know that maintaining the delicate balance they worked to achieve requires vigilance over time," wrote Maria Colacurcio, CEO of software start-up Syndio Solutions, and Rob Porcarelli, the company's chief legal officer, in an article in *Medium*.[134] "Unless companies undertake efforts to identify the underlying policies, practices, and manager behaviors that led to those disparities to begin with, those gaps will reappear quickly and regularly."

Taking a Regulatory Approach

Multiple countries (including the United Kingdom, France, Germany, Iceland, and Canada) have passed laws that attempt to end gender pay gaps, either by making it illegal to pay women less than men or by mandating companies to publish pay gap information and to outline the steps they have taken to eliminate gaps.[135] "Perhaps the most aggressive approach to date has come out of Iceland," according to a 2018 article in *International Labor and Employment Law*. "Despite already being considered one of the world's most gender-equal countries, Iceland's new pay equity law, which took effect in January 2018, requires that any company with at least 25 employees prove to an external auditor that it provides equal pay to its employees." After analyzing a company's data, the auditor decides whether to certify the company as being in compliance with Icelandic law.

Without laws like these in the United States, the gender pay gap may exist indefinitely. The Institute for Women's Policy Research estimates that if change continues at the same slow pace as it has for the past 50 years, it will take until the year 2059 for women to earn the same as men.[136] "For women of color, the rate of change is even slower: Hispanic women will have to wait until 2224, and black women will wait until 2119 for equal pay." This should be unacceptable to all of us, especially Dignity Mindset leaders who believe that everyone in an organization has the same worth and the same fundamental human needs as everyone else.

Creating transparency around pay data is a crucial first step toward ending the gender pay gap. Hopefully we're moving toward that in the U.S. As of this writing, a federal judge has ruled that companies with more than 100 employees will have to submit pay data to the Federal government that's broken down by sex, race, and ethnicity; however, appeals are being considered and compliance dates are up in the air. Even so, equal pay advocates see it as a first step. Emily Martin, vice president for education and workplace justice for the National Women's Law Center, one of the groups that sued to get the wage information included in the ruling, said, "In order to have equal and fair pay, employees need more information about their employers' pay policies. So, this is one step, but it's not the last step."[137]

Providing Voluntary Transparency

Of course, companies don't have to wait for regulations that push them to be more transparent. Some organizations are already exercising transparency about pay and hiring, and it's bringing positive results. For example, Starbucks has made a public commitment to pay equity and considers transparency a core part of its approach since 2008, when it began its companywide compensation study program. In 2018, Starbucks announced that it had reached 100% pay equity for partners of all genders and races performing similar work across the U.S.[138] The company is continuing to work on equity in its global operations.

Starbucks said it reached its 100% goal in the U.S. through the use of a range of tools and best practices for preventing disparities, which include a calculator to objectively determine target starting pay ranges based on a candidate's experience and statistical analysis of raises and bonuses to make sure they haven't been impacted by bias. (The company lists its tools and best practices on its website, starbucks.com, so others can copy its success.) In addition, Starbucks has stopped asking job candidates for salary histories, is transparent with employees about pay ranges, and encourages employees to ask about or discuss wages without fear of discrimination or retaliation. "I want our partners to know what we're committing to so they can hold us accountable," said Sara Bowen, an attorney who leads the Starbucks Inclusion, Diversity, Equity, and Accessibility team.

Transparency can make companies more appealing to employees; a true commitment to dignity and diversity that plays out in your organization's words, actions, and policies can really pay off in terms of how your organization is viewed by current and potential workers as well as the business community at large.

Accenture, which was named the #1 company on the 2018 Thomson Reuters Diversity & Inclusion Index—which recognizes the 100 most diverse and inclusive companies in the world—is committed to transparency. According to Accenture, the company was "the first professional services company to voluntarily publish comprehensive workforce demographics— including gender, ethnicity, persons with disabilities, and veterans—in the United States."[139] The company set a goal of having women comprise 50% of its global workforce by 2025; today, the company is transparent about the fact that women comprise 41% of the company's workforce and 45% of new hires.

Augmented Decision-Making: Using AI as a Measurement Tool

We've discussed in this book the ways in which technology has fed into bias—for example, in misogynistic video games and in the gender wage/ opportunity gaps in the tech industry. But as we've examined the various tools that can drive dignity, inclusion, and diversity in workplaces, we've also seen many examples of the script being flipped: Instead of adding to the bias burden of women and other groups, many innovative entrepreneurs are using technology to help fix these problems, rather than add to them.

As we look at measurement, artificial intelligence (AI) stands out as a useful technology to identify (measure) and reduce (manage) bias. An application known as augmented decision-making—using AI to improve human decisions—can address equity in the hiring and other processes, not by being blind to bias by recognizing it.

A nice example of this comes from Pipeline, a Denver-based startup. Pipeline offers a proprietary SaaS platform that uses AI to assess, address, and take action against gender biases within organizations.[140] Through direct integration with an organization's cloud-based human capital management system, according to the company, Pipeline can analyze data based on a series of events and make recommendations that support improved financial performance for the organization, as well as growth for the individual. It also pairs improved gender equity with financial metrics.[141]

"Gender equity is not only a social issue, it is a massive economic opportunity," said Katica Roy, Pipeline's CEO and founder, who is very active in gender equity issues.[142]

The Grit Scale: A New Way to Predict Success

You've probably noticed that some employees demonstrate a tenacity that's so strong, you wish you could bottle it up and feed it to everyone else in the company. That passionate, persevering spirit is known as grit, according to Angela Duckworth, a professor of psychology at the University of Pennsylvania and the founder and CEO of Character Lab, a nonprofit whose mission is to advance the science and practice of character development.

Duckworth created a tool called the Grit Scale to measure grit, which she defines as the "passion and perseverance for long-term goals."[143] Duckworth details her research into grit in her bestselling book, *Grit: The Power of Passion and Perseverance*. As Duckworth explains, "Grit isn't talent. Grit isn't luck. Grit isn't how intensely, for the moment, you want something. Instead, grit is about having what some researchers call an ultimate concern—a goal you care about so much that it organizes and gives meaning to almost everything you do. And grit is holding steadfast to that goal. Even when you fall down." Although talent and luck are components of success, Duckworth believes that "in the very long run, I think grit may matter as least as much, if not more."

Her tool, the Grit Scale (available in her book or on her website, angeladuckworth.com) measures grit. After answering the questions on the scale, users find out how they score in comparison with other American adults in a recent study. Leaders can use the Grit Scale to identify high-potential talent, especially among employees who are not readily visible to decision-makers and the straight white men in the core power structure.

Trust-Measuring Surveys

As we discussed at length in Tool #5: Take Trust to the Next Level, building trust is crucial in a dignity-driven workplace. To make sure you're properly managing trust, you must measure it. One way to do this is to utilize trust-measuring surveys that ask questions such as:

+ Do leaders ask for and listen to feedback about trustworthiness?
+ Do leaders trust employees to be both highly competent and to have high integrity?
+ Do leaders work to ensure that networks within the organization are open and welcoming?
+ Do employees feel comfortable communicating in a full and honest way with all their leaders, as opposed to just a subset of them?
+ Do employees proactively and regularly seek out colleagues to create connections and build trusting relationships?

Carefully designed surveys can go a long way toward identifying trust gaps and defining directions for future work on trust for leaders, employers, and the organization as a whole.

Dignity Dashboards

Companies and nonprofits use organizational dashboards to monitor and measure a wide range of mission-critical performance metrics. An organizational dashboard helps guide executives and employees as they work to improve performance and align fully with corporate goals and values. Dashboards also allow organizations to collect important data that can help inform future goals.

As you implement Dignity Mindset-based approaches to your business, consider creating a Dignity Dashboard to monitor and measure performance related to the tools we've discussed in this book. Keep in mind that a Dignity Dashboard should not be a separate initiative, but a central part of your organization's primary dash-boarding process. For example, inclusion would be one dial on your dashboard that's equal to other mission-critical concentrations such as profitability or overall performance.

A Dignity Dashboard can include some of the questions listed here. (And incidentally, these questions can also be included in performance management and compensation tools.)

Dignity Dashboard Questions About the CEO:

Do I trust the CEO to be fair?
Does the CEO:

+ Create a culture that ensures I am seen and recognized for my work?
+ Consistently message the importance of inclusion, and hold herself/ himself accountable for having an inclusive and engaged team?
+ Hold the management team accountable for creating an inclusive workforce by engaging diverse individuals in the central work of the business?
+ Have a method to learn about and address micro-aggressions occurring in the trenches of everyday work?
+ Hold direct reports accountable to amplify and operationalize key messages, including about fairness and inclusion?

Is the CEO:

+ Working to close the pay gap in our company?
+ Transparent about inequities in our company and what she/he is doing to resolve them?
+ Consistently transparent about how talent decisions/selections are made?

Dignity Dashboard Questions About Managers:

Do I trust that my manager has my back?
Does my manager:

+ Display ongoing commitment to gender equity for women of all colors?
+ Operate under the values of a Dignity Mindset, with the belief that everyone in the organization has the same value and fundamental human needs as everyone else?
+ Make it her/his business to ensure that everyone in our group upholds the values of a Dignity Mindset?
+ Ensure that women of all colors receive the same visibility to upper management as do the men on our team?
+ Actively coach me as part of supporting my success?
+ Actively discourage behaviors that exclude me (both active and passive) at work and outside of work?
+ Listen when I have concerns about micro-aggressions?
+ Care about me?

Dignity Dashboard Questions About Co-workers:

Do I trust my co-workers to have my back?
Do I see examples of bias based on gender, race, or other factors in my company?

Do my co-workers:

+ Value me as a part of the team?
+ Communicate honestly and constructively with me?
+ Provide honest, constructive feedback to me or about me to others?
+ Ask me for feedback?
+ Listen to me?
+ Ensure I'm included equally in work-related dialogue, meetings, etc.?
+ Reach around or over me in an effort to serve their personal gendas?

Creating a Dignity Dashboard sends a powerful message about your commitment to operate with a Dignity Mindset. Giving dignity a place equal to other crucial success measures not only demonstrates its value but improves the likelihood of it being taken seriously by everyone in the organization.

GenderAvenger: Bringing Women's Voices Forward

Have you attended a conference with all male speakers? Have you observed (or perhaps participated in) panels with little or no female participation? It's a real issue, and one clever and outstanding set of tools to level the field in conferences comes from GenderAvenger (GA). This volunteer organization is working tirelessly to ensure that women's voices are represented in the public dialog, especially in business and academia. Launched in 2014 by cofounders Gina Glantz and Susan Askew, GA uses "the power of one simple gesture: the count" to track "how women and women of color are represented (or not) in the public sphere." GA believes that counting "creates awareness and becomes a powerful visual for change."[144]

The GA Tally App enables users to record and share gender balance (or imbalance) they see every day—at conferences, on television, in magazines, and so on. The app makes it easy for users to track who's present at an event such as a conference by submitting the number of men, women, and women of color who are participating. Users can upload their own photos or let the GA Tally App generate pie charts that users can post on social media. Or, users can track the time participants spend talking by using a two-button system on the app. Live reporting allows those in the audience to document, for example, when one or two males take up the majority of the airtime on a panel.

The GA Stamp of Approval is designed to acknowledge and celebrate conference and event organizers that demonstrate a commitment to inclusion on stage, according to GA.

Stamps of Approval are awarded to public events that meet one of the following criteria:

+ Gold: 40%+ women, of whom 50% are women of color
+ Silver: 40%+ women, of whom 40% are women of color
+ Bronze: 40%+ women, of whom 30% are women of color[145]

Part of GA's power comes from the fact that it is using a new kind of measurement to bring real-time accountability to previously closed shops and in all kinds of places and sectors. The impact of measuring and reporting on speaker gender data at conferences— including major ones like the Annual Consumer Electronics Show (CES)—has caused event organizers to make major changes from one year to the next. In 2017 GA's criticism of CES for having an all-male speaker lineup received lots of negative media attention. CES took note, and a year later, CES received GA's Gold Stamp of Approval for "a diverse lineup of keynote and featured speakers" for the 2019 show that included 45% women, 60% of whom were women of color.[146] "We look forward to a time when organizations meet GenderAvenger's standards without the necessity of public shaming," Glantz wrote in a letter to CES organizers. "As CES has shown, it's really not that hard."

GA's commitment is serious, but it has fun along the way, taking a tongue-in-cheek approach to shining the light of measurement on gender bias. Some of the ratings GA gives to various events include "a thunderstorm of gender inequality," "cloudy with a chance of patriarchy," and "the present and future are bright." It's a unique and powerful team and approach.

GA offers users access to a full toolkit of equity tools, including action alerts about good, bad, and ugly gender equity news. For example, an April 2019 alert gave users a series of numbers about gender representation in the *New Yorker* in the first few months of the year, including the number of cartoons drawn by women (19) and men (36). A May 2019 action alert revealed that the FinTech World Forum 2019 speaker list included 13 men and no women. Now that's a thunderstorm of gender inequality.

As a dignity-driven leader, perhaps you'll consider signing the GA pledge found on the organization's website, GenderAvenger.com. The pledge is simple: "I will not serve as a panelist at a public conference where there are no women on the panel." (A panel consists of three or more people.) Signing this pledge and holding yourself, your executive team, and your employees to it is a perfect way to demonstrate that you're operating in alignment with the values of a Dignity Mindset. While you're at it, why not sign the ParityPledge at parity.org? Parity's goal is that organizations "commit to interview and consider at least one qualified woman for every open role, VP and higher, including the Csuite and the board." According to Parity, a long list of companies have taken the pledge, including Athenahealth, Nasdaq, Oracle, Adobe, Cisco, and Best Buy.[147]

Measure It to Manage It

Measurement won't guarantee success, but it does make it far more likely. Measuring performance through the collection and analysis of data helps improve outcomes and highlight shortcomings. Likewise, reporting the results of your measurements creates transparency, and because transparency leads to trust, it makes space for dignity and diversity to take root and bloom.

A Dignity Mindset is a framework that is built around the belief that everyone in an organization has the same worth and the same fundamental human needs as everyone else. You've made a commitment to dignity; objective measurement allows you to gauge your progress. With that data in hand, you can celebrate victories and establish updated goals for the future.

CONCLUSION

A Note to the Good Guys

"Fight for the things that you care about but do it in
a way that will lead others to join you."[148]

— Supreme Court Justice Ruth Bader Ginsburg

We've taken a close look in this book at the many ways that hegemonic masculinity and bias against women harms individuals, organizations, and our society as a whole. And we've explored a comprehensive collection of Dignity Mindset tools that enlightened leaders can use to steer their organizations toward an inclusive, equal future that recognizes and supports the belief that everyone in an organization has the same worth and the same fundamental human needs as everyone else.

If you're a man, parts of this book may not have been easy to read. That's why I want to conclude with an acknowledgement to the men who choose to step out of their comfort zones to ally with women to work toward making this world a fairer, safer, and more equitable place, and to speak out when they see and hear things that don't honor women.

I know there are a lot of you good guys out there in the world. You feel stress, pressure, and the force of change. You try to do the right thing: Each day you get up, get dressed, go to work, contribute your best to your organization, and do your most to prove yourself and create impact at work. And yet, you may find yourself missing your kids' afterschool games, wishing you had spent time at home when they were born, wondering how you will survive the next round of layoffs, shaking your head when you read about heart attack and suicide rates going up among your peers, and feeling concerned that you can't always live up to your own high expectations.

And on top of it all, you may wonder what you did to make everyone so pissed off at you for being part of the power structure.

It's a frustrating and difficult position. But I urge you to lean forward on your toes, rather than digging in your heels, to embrace a Dignity Mindset with all of your energy and enthusiasm. It's not just the right thing to do— it's also the best possible way to stay relevant in a changing corporate world.

Of this I have no doubt: If taking a stand for equity feels personally risky, it's nothing compared to the career risk you are taking by resisting diversity. The world is changing; being on the wrong side of this one is your best guarantee you'll be left behind.

What's more, supporting and enabling gender equality is good for men as well as women. As equality advocate and author Michael Kaufman writes, "There are so many of us, so many men, who are now realizing these changes stand to make our lives better, too."[149] I stand with Kaufman as he calls on men to stand up for women: "It's time for men to join the fight for gender equality."[150]

I think so often of the incredibly nice gentlemen I meet at airport gates, all of us exhausted at 10:30 or 11 at night, standing in line, waiting for delayed planes, fending off starvation with stale chips from airport newsstands. I can't tell you how many times, my back screaming in pain at the end of a long day running seminars, that I have asked a nice guy to help me negotiate the boarding gauntlet because even over a year after back surgery, the night ride home can be a pretty tough challenge. I can't tell you how often these gentlemen put my bag in the overhead compartment without asking and quietly move to retrieve it for me at the end of the flight. It happens all the time. They often don't say much, but they always keep an eye out to see if I need help. How I value these men and all the men in my personal and professional life who are guided by a Dignity Mindset, and who add immeasurably to my life experience.

This book is for all the wonderful men in the world. Let's change this toxic, mythologic, arbitrary imbalance of power once and for all so life can be better for *all* of us. If we work together and take care of each other, we will improve the very nature of our shared existence. A candle loses nothing by lighting another candle. When we each share our light, we all shine.

ABOUT THE AUTHOR

Susan Hodgkinson, a trailblazer in personal branding, founded The Personal Brand Company in 1994. She is a leadership development expert, award-winning executive coach, and keynote speaker. Hodgkinson was the first practitioner in the U.S. to combine 15 years of a corporate marketing and branding approach to developing leaders, and the first to build a leadership development model—The 5 P's of Leadership Brand®—fusing the two disciplines.

Hodgkinson was the first practitioner in the U.S. to create a leadership development model that incorporated the needs and issues of women and people of color into the mainstream framework, vs. creating a separate framework for these talent pools. She has coached hundreds of executives one on one in the U.S., Western Europe, Latin America, Canada, and India. Her work with high-potential, high-performing women leaders, including many women of color, has made her a foremost authority on gender and inclusion, and intersectional development in the U.S.

She works with thousands of professionals in a diverse array of businesses who know they must strategically manage their own professional learning, leadership development, and personal brand to succeed—for their companies and themselves.

The Dignity Mindset is Hodgkinson's second book. Her first book, *The Leader's Edge: Using Personal Branding to Drive Performance and Profit*, has sold more than 50,000 copies worldwide and received the Pinnacle Book Achievement Award.

Hodgkinson is a recipient of India's World HRD Congress Leadership Award, and a member of the Forbes Coaches Council. Her work has most recently been featured in *The Wall Street Journal*, *The New York Times*, *The Indian Express*, *The Detroit Free Press*, and *Essence Magazine*. She holds an MBA from Simmons School of Management and is on the Executive Education faculty there, at Boston's The Partnership, and at other business schools and Leadership Institutes.

To book Susan Hodgkinson for your next Keynote: info@thepersonal brandcompany.com

ENDNOTES

1 "Women on Corporate Boards." Catalyst. December 21, 2018. https://www.catalyst.org/knowledge/womencorporate-boards#footnote33_wkynwps

2 Kaufman, Michael. "The Time Has Come: Why Men Must Join the Gender Equality Revolution." Counterpoint, 2019, page 33.

3 "Pay Equity Information." National Committee on Pay Equity. https://www.pay-equity.org/info-time.html

4 "Fast Facts." National Center for Education Statistics. https://nces.ed.gov/fastfacts/display.asp?id=372

5 "The Share of Female CEOs in the Fortune 500 Dropped by 25% in 2018." Fortune. May 21, 2018. http://fortune.com/2018/05/21/women-fortune-500-2018/

6 "Women on Corporate Boards." Catalyst. December 21, 2018. https://www.catalyst.org/knowledge/womencorporate-boards#footnote33_wkynwps

7 "Wanted: 3,732 Women to Govern Corporate America." Bloomberg Businessweek. March 21, 2019. https://www.bloomberg.com/graphics/2019-women-on-boards/

8 "Gender Discrimination Comes in Many Forms for Today's Working Women." Pew Research Center. https://www.pewresearch.org/fact-tank/2017/12/14/gender-discrimination-comes-in-many-forms-for-todaysworking-women/

9 "Sexual Harassment: What Do the Polls Say?" Forbes, January 16, 2018. https://www.forbes.com/sites/bowmanmarsico/2018/01/16/sexual-harassment-what-do-the-pollssay/#5d844ea55ac0

10 "Women on Corporate Boards." Catalyst. December 21, 2018. https://www.catalyst.org/knowledge/womencorporate-boards#footnote33_wkynwps

11 "Why MSCI?" MSCI. https://www.msci.com/our-story

12 "The Tipping Point: Women on Boards and Financial Performance." MSCI. https://www.msci.com/www/research-paper/the-tipping-point-women-on-0538947986

13 Blum, Robert et al. "It Begins at 10: How Gender Expectations Shape Early Adolescence Around the World." Journal of Adolescent Health. 2017 Oct;61(4 Suppl): S3-S4. https://www.jahonline.org/article/S1054139X(17)30355-5/fulltext

14 "In China, Highly Educated Women are Mocked as a Sexless 'Third Gender.'" Quartz. January 29, 2014. https://qz.com/312464/in-china-highly-educated-women-are-mocked-as-a-sexless-third-gender/

15 "The Silence About Incest Needs to be Broken." Revista Envio. http://www.envio.org.ni/articulo/1445

16 "Child Sexual Abuse Statistics." The National Center for Victims of Crime. http://victimsofcrime.org/media/reporting-on-child-sexual-abuse/child-sexual-abuse-statistics

17 "The Wage Gap for Women of Color Widened in 2017." National Women's Law Center. https://nwlc.org/blog/the-wage-gap-for-women-of-color-widened-in-2017/

18 "Gender Pay Gap Starts with Kids in America." BusyKid. https://busykid.com/2018/06/29/gender-pay-gap-startswith-kids-in-america/

19 "Sexual Harassment: What Do the Polls Say?" Forbes, January 16, 2018. https://www.forbes.com/sites/bowmanmarsico/2018/01/16/sexual-harassment-what-do-the-pollssay/#5d844ea55ac0

20 "It's Good to be the Queen, but it's Easier to be the King." McKinsey & Company. https://www.mckinsey.com/featured-insights/leadership/its-good-to-be-the-queen-but-its-easier-being-the-king

21 Mulvey, Laura. "Visual Pleasure in Narrative Cinema." http://www.luxonline.org.uk/articles/visual_pleasure_and_narrative_cinema%28printversion%29.html

22 "Bechdel Test Movie List: Statistics and Graphs." Bechdeltest.com. https://bechdeltest.com/statistics/

23 "10 Surprising Films that Fail the Bechdel Test." The Daily Edge. https://www.dailyedge.ie/films-that-dont-passthe-bechdel-test-surprising-3894296-Mar2018/

24 "Box Office: 'Captain Marvel' Flies to Historic $153M in U.S., $455M Globally." The Hollywood Reporter, March 10, 2019. https://www.hollywoodreporter.com/heat-vision/box-office-captain-marvel-opens-historic-153m-us455m-globally-1193585

25 "Oscars: No Women Nominated for Best Director—Again." Hollywood Reporter, January 24, 2017. https://www.hollywoodreporter.com/news/oscars-no-women-nominated-best-director-again-967284

26 "Study: Female-Led Movies Make More Money at the Box Office." Fast Company, December 11, 2018. https://www.fastcompany.com/90279703/study-female-led-movies-make-more-money-at-the-box-office

27 "Gender Bias on Wikipedia." Wikipedia. Accessed March 13, 2019. https://en.wikipedia.org/wiki/Gender_bias_on_Wikipedia

28 "Gender Across Wikipedia Project Contributors in 2018, Weighted." Wikipedia. https://en.wikipedia.org/wiki/Gender_bias_on_Wikipedia#/media/File:LE15_Gender_overall_in_2018.png

29 "History Has a Massive Gender Bias. We'll Settle for Fixing Wikipedia." Washington Post, February 17, 2019. https://www.washingtonpost.com/lifestyle/style/history-has-a-massive-gender-bias-well-settle-for-fixingwikipedia/2019/02/15/b2537640-3163-11e9-86ab-5d02109aeb01_story.html?utm_term=.a38dceb18785

30 "The Best DJs in the World Right Now." Ranker. https://www.ranker.com/crowdranked-list/the-best-djs-in-theworld-1. Accessed March 14, 2019.

31 "The Fearless Girl Statue Finds a New Home: At the New York Stock Exchange." New York Times, December 10, 2018. https://www.nytimes.com/2018/12/10/nyregion/fearless-girl-statue-stock-exchange-.html

32 "Pissed Off Artist Adds Statue of Urinating Dog Next to 'Fearless Girl.'" New York Post, May 29, 2017. https://nypost.com/2017/05/29/pissed-off-artist-adds-statue-of-urinating-dog-next-to-fearless-girl/

33 Johnson, Paula A. et al. "Sex-Specific Medical Research: Why Women's Health Can't Wait." Brigham and Women's Hospital, The Boston Foundation, and The George Washington University, 2014. https://www.brighamandwomens.org/assets/BWH/womens-health/pdfs/ConnorsReportFINAL.pdf

34 Mehta, Laxmi S. et al. "Acute Myocardial Infarction in Women." American Heart Association, 2016. https://www.ahajournals.org/doi/pdf/10.1161/cir.0000000000000351?sid=beb5f268-4205-4e62-be8f3caec4c4d9b7&

35 "She Wanted to Do Her Research. He Wanted to Talk 'Feelings.'" New York Times, March 4, 2016. https://www.nytimes.com/2016/03/06/opinion/sunday/she-wanted-to-do-her-research-he-wanted-to-talkfeelings.html

36 "The State of Online Gaming 2019." Limelight Network. https://www.limelight.com/resources/whitepaper/state-of-online-gaming-2019/

37 "This Violent Videogame Has Made More Money Than Any Movie Ever." MarketWatch, April 9, 2018. https://www.marketwatch.com/story/this-violent-videogame-has-made-more-money-than-any-movie-ever-201804-06

38 "The 26 Most Messed Up Things You Can Do in Grand Theft Auto." TheGamer.com, November 23, 2017. https://www.thegamer.com/the-most-messed-up-things-you-can-do-in-grand-theft-auto/

39 "Gaming's Toxic Men, Explained." Polygon, July 25, 2018. https://www.polygon.com/2018/7/25/17593516/video-game-culture-toxic-men-explained

40 "Resolution on Violent Video Games." American Psychological Association. https://www.apa.org/about/policy/violent-video-games

41 "Video Games Can Activate the Brain's Pleasure Circuits." Psychology Today, October 25, 2011. https://www.psychologytoday.com/us/blog/the-

compass-pleasure/201110/video-games-can-activate-the-brainspleasure-circuits-0

42 "What is Gaming Disorder?" MedicalNewsToday, July 16, 2018. https://www.medicalnewstoday.com/articles/322478.php

43 "Video Games May Change Brain and Behavior, Review Finds." World Federation of Neurology, June 23, 2017. https://www.wfneurology.org/2017-06-23-sci-news

44 "Video Games are Now a Legitimate High School Sport." CNN, March 18, 2019. https://www.cnn.com/2019/03/18/tech/esports-varsity-arena/index.html

45 "Gaming's Toxic Men, Explained." Polygon, July 25, 2018. https://www.polygon.com/2018/7/25/17593516/video-game-culture-toxic-men-explained

46 "About Feminist Frequency." Feminist Frequency. https://feministfrequency.com/about/

47 "Girls Who Play Video Games 3x More Likely to Study STEM Degrees." Big Think, October 23, 2018. https://bigthink.com/culture-religion/girl-gamers-pursue-stem-degrees?rebelltitem=3#rebelltitem3

48 Clance, Pauline R, and Imes, Suzanne A. "The Imposter Phenomenon in High-Achieving Women: Dynamics and Therapeutic Intervention." Fall 1978. Psychotherapy Theory, Research and Practice. 15 (3): 241–247. http://www.paulineroseclance.com/pdf/ip_high_achieving_women.pdf

49 "How to Handle Imposter Syndrome." MedicalNewsToday, reviewed May 4, 2018. https://www.medicalnewstoday.com/articles/321730.php

50 "Online Harassment 2017." Pew Research Center. https://www.pewinternet.org/2017/07/11/onlineharassment-2017/

51 "Study: Excessive Social Media Use Could Harm Female Self-Esteem." United Press International, May 5, 2018. https://www.upi.com/Study-Excessive-social-media-use-could-harm-female-self-esteem/2131525500974/

52 Twenge, JM et al. "Increases in Depressive Symptoms, Suicide-Related Outcomes, and Suicide Rates Among U.S. Adolescents after 2010 and Links to Increased New Media Screen Time." Clinical Psychological Science, November 14, 2017. https://journals.sagepub.com/doi/abs/10.1177/2167702617723376?journalCode=cpxa

53 "How Much Time Do People Spend on Social Media?" SocialMedia Today. https://www.socialmediatoday.com/marketing/how-much-time-do-people-spend-social-media-infographic

54 "The Gap Table: Analyzing the Gender Gap in Equity." Carta. September 17, 2018. https://carta.com/blog/gaptable/

55 Kaufman, Michael. "The Time Has Come: Why Men Must Join the Gender Equity Revolution." Page 47-48.

56 Kaufman, Michael. "Man Talk: What Every Guy Oughta/Gotta Know About Good Relationships." http://www.michaelkaufman.com/wp-content/uploads/2016/01/ManTalk-2016-online-version.pdf

57 Kaufman, Michael. "Hot Topics: Sexual Harassment on Campus." http://www.globalspeakers.com/blog/gsa-hottopics-sexual-harassment-on-campus-by-michael-kaufman/

58 Kaufman, Michael. "Man Talk: What Every Guy Oughta/Gotta Know About Good Relationships." http://www.michaelkaufman.com/wp-content/uploads/2016/01/ManTalk-2016-online-version.pdf

59 "Faculty Salaries Up 3%." Inside Higher Ed, April 11, 2018. https://www.insidehighered.com/news/2018/04/11/aaups-annual-report-faculty-compensation-takes-salarycompression-and-more

60 "Gender Pay Gap Persists Across Faculty Ranks." The Chronicle of Higher Education. https://www.chronicle.com/article/Gender-Pay-Gap-Persists-Across/239553

61 "How Silicon Valley's Sexist 'Bro Culture' Affects Everyone—And How to Fix It." Business Insider, Feb. 15, 2018. https://www.businessinsider.com/emily-chang-silicon-valley-sexism-exposed-in-new-book-brotopia-2018-2

62 "Why the Gender Discrimination Lawsuit Against Nike is So Significant." Vox, August 15, 2018. https://www.vox.com/2018/8/15/17683484/nike-women-gender-pay-discrimination-lawsuit

63 "2012 Harvard Men's Soccer Team Produced Sexually Explicit 'Scouting Report' on Female Recruits." Harvard Crimson, October 25, 2016. https://www.thecrimson.com/article/2016/10/25/harvard-mens-soccer-2012-report/

64 "Snapchat CEO Evan Spiegel 'Mortified' by Leaked Frat Emails." Los Angeles Times, May 28, 2014. https://www.latimes.com/business/technology/la-fi-tn-snapchat-evan-spiegel-20140528-story.html

65 "Snap Paid Settlements to Women Who Alleged Discrimination." Wall Street Journal, March 6, 2019. https://www.wsj.com/articles/snap-layoffs-led-to-payouts-to-ousted-female-employees-11551877200

66 Thurston, Rebecca C. et al. "Association of Sexual Harassment and Sexual Assault with Midlife Women's Mental and Physical Health. *JAMA Intern Med.* 2019;179(1):48–53. https://jamanetwork.com/journals/jamainternalmedicine/article-abstract/2705688

67 Kaufman, Michael. "The Time Has Come: Why Men Must Join the Gender Equality Revolution." Page 61.

68 Kaufman, Michael. "The Time Has Come: Why Men Must Join the Gender Equality Revolution." Page 58.

69 Sawyer, Jack. "On Male Liberation." Academia. August-September-October 1970. https://www.academia.edu/33743560/On_Male_Liberation

70 "Salesforce Leadership." Salesforce. https://www.salesforce.com/company/leadership/

71 "About Salesforce." Salesforce. https://www.salesforce.com/products/what-is-salesforce/

72 "Leading By Example to Close the Gender Pay Gap." CBSNews.com. https://www.cbsnews.com/news/salesforceceo-marc-benioff-leading-by-example-to-close-the-gender-pay-gap/

73 "People Announces 50 Companies That Care." Meredith MediaRoom. http://meredith.mediaroom.com/2018-07-25-PEOPLE-Announces-50-Companies-That-Care

74 "2019 Salesforce Equal Pay Update." Salesforce. https://www.salesforce.com/blog/2019/04/equal-pay-update2019.html

75 Troiano, Emily V. "Sharing Failures Leads to Learning Opportunities for All." https://www.catalyst.org/2018/12/19/sharing-failures-leads-to-learning-opportunities-for-all/

76 "The Origin of the Human Library." The Human Library. http://humanlibrary.org/about-the-human-library/

77 "Virtual Reality Tested by NFL As a Tool to Confront Racism, Sexism." USA Today. April 10, 2016. https://www.usatoday.com/story/tech/news/2016/04/08/virtual-reality-tested-tool-confront-racismsexism/82674406/

78 "Virtual Reality Can Help Make People More Compassionate Compared to Other Media, New Study Finds." Stanford News. October 17, 2018. https://news.stanford.edu/2018/10/17/virtual-reality-can-help-make-peopleempathetic/

79 "Equal Reality." http://www.equalreality.com/index

80 "Follow Her Lead: What Women Bring to Business." The Atlantic, Sponsored by Deloitte. https://www.theatlantic.com/sponsored/deloitte-2019/follow-her-lead/3052/

81 "Catalyst Launches #BiasCorrect Campaign to Tackle Unconscious Gender Bias in the Workplace on International Women's Day." Catalyst. March 7, 2019. https://www.catalyst.org/media-release/biascorrect-iwd-internationalwomens-day/

82 "Empathy Quiz." Greater Good Magazine. https://greatergood.berkeley.edu/quizzes/take_quiz/empathy

83 "Key Findings from the Women in the Workplace 2018 Report." LeanIn.Org and McKinsey. https://leanin.org/women-in-the-workplace

84 "Unconscious Bias." Catalyst. https://www.catalyst.org/topics/unconscious-bias/

85 "About Us." Project Implicit. https://implicit.harvard.edu/implicit/aboutus.html

86 "Select a Test." Project Implicit. https://implicit.harvard.edu/implicit/selectatest.html

87 Kanter, Rosabeth Moss. Men and Women of the Corporation. Page 48.

88 "The Share of Female CEOs in the Fortune 500 Dropped by 25% in 2018." Fortune. May 21, 2018. http://fortune.com/2018/05/21/women-fortune-500-2018/

89 "Binders Full of Women." Wikipedia. https://en.wikipedia.org/wiki/Binders_full_of_women

90 "Delivering Through Diversity." McKinsey & Company. https://www.mckinsey.com/businessfunctions/organization/our-insights/delivering-through-diversity

91 "Women in the Workplace 2018." McKinsey & Company. Page 6 (illustration). https://womenintheworkplace.com/

92 "Women in the Workplace 2018." McKinsey & Company. Page 4. https://womenintheworkplace.com/

93 "Female Recruiters Leading the Charge to Close the Gender Equity Gap." Scout Exchange. https://www.goscoutgo.com/female-recruiters-leading-the-charge-to-close-the-gender-equity-gap/

94 "Female Recruiters Leading the Charge to Close the Gender Equity Gap." Scout Exchange. https://www.goscoutgo.com/female-recruiters-leading-the-charge-to-close-the-gender-equity-gap/

95 "Gender Insights Report." LinkedIn. https://business.linkedin.com/talent-solutions/blog/diversity/2019/howwomen-find-jobs-gender-report

96 "Rethinking Your Gender Equity Strategy." Scout Slide Deck.

97 "Our Story." Scout. https://www.goscoutgo.com/about-us/our-story/

98 Mead, Ursula. "Care About Gender Equity? Ask Hiring Managers These 5 Questions." Fast Company. May 18, 2018. https://www.fastcompany.com/40573295/care-about-gender-equality-ask-hiring-managers-these-5questions

99 "Diverse Commencement Speakers Won't Change the Fact That There's A Lack of Female Leadership in Higher Ed." GenderAvenger. April 26, 2019. https://www.GenderAvenger.com/blog/commencement-speakers-womenhigher-ed

100 "The Speed of Trust Executive Book Summary." University of Colorado. https://www.cu.edu/sites/default/files/ExecSummaries-The_Speed_of_Trust.pdf

101 "Announcing the Second Annual Great Place to Work for All Leadership Awards." Press release. February 27, 2019. https://www.greatplacetowork.com/press-releases/announcing-the-2nd-annual-great-place-to-work-for-allleadership-awards

102 "9 Reasons High-Trust Culture Means Better Business." Great Place to Work. https://www.greatplacetowork.com/business-case-poll

103 "Study: Could Trust Cost You a Generation of Talent? Trust in the Workforce." Ernst & Young. https://www.ey.com/gl/en/about-us/our-people-and-culture/ey-global-study-trust-in-the-workplace

104 "Women in the Workplace 2018." McKinsey & Company. https://www.mckinsey.com/featured-insights/genderequality/women-in-the-workplace-2018

105 "The Simple Truth About the Gender Pay Gap." American Association of University Women (AAUW). Fall 2018. https://www.aauw.org/aauw_check/pdf_download/show_pdf.php?file=simple-truth-one-pager

106 "Black Women Disproportionately Experience Workplace Sexual Harassment, New NWLC Report Reveals." National Women's Law Center, August 2, 2018. https://nwlc.org/press-releases/black-women-disproportionatelyexperience-workplace-sexual-harassment-new-nwlc-report-reveals/

107 "WorldatWork Survey Reveals Broad Pay Transparency, A Hallmark of Pay Equity, Remains Uncommon." WorldatWork. February 19, 2019. https://www.worldatwork.org/press-room/worldatwork-survey-reveals-broadpay-transparency-a-hallmark-of-pay-equity-remains-uncommon

108 "Pay Equity Information." National Committee on Pay Equity. https://www.pay-equity.org/info-time.html

109 "The Wage Gap for Women of Color Widened in 2017." National Women's Law Center. https://nwlc.org/blog/the-wage-gap-for-women-of-color-widened-in-2017/

110 "The Simple Truth About the Gender Pay Gap." American Association of University Women (AAUW). Fall 2018. https://www.aauw.org/aauw_check/pdf_download/show_pdf.php?file=simple-truth-one-pager

111 "Why Diversity and Inclusion Matter." Catalyst. August 1, 2018. https://www.catalyst.org/knowledge/whydiversity-and-inclusion-matter#footnote20_72y5nz2

112 "Highest-Paid TV Actresses 2018." Variety. October 25, 2018. https://www.forbes.com/sites/natalierobehmed/2018/10/25/highest-paid-tv-actresses-2018-sofia-vergara-topsranking-again-with-42-5-million/#6b0910244799

113 "Black Women: Ready to Lead." Center for Talent Innovation. http://www.talentinnovation.org/publication.cfm?publication=1460

114 "Study Explores Black Women's Appetite for Leadership." Center for Talent Innovation. Press release. https://www.talentinnovation.org/_private/assets/BlackWomenReadyToLead_pressrelease-CTI-4_21_2015.pdf

115 Bacon, Terry R. "The Power of Networking." http://www.theelementsofpower.com/power-and-influenceblog/the-power-of-networking/

116 "New Survey Reveals 85% of All Jobs are Filled Via Networking." LinkedIn. February 29, 2016. https://www.linkedin.com/pulse/new-survey-reveals-85-all-jobs-filled-via-networking-lou-adler/

117 "How Long Does It Take to Advance Women? 36 Minutes a Week." JPMorgan Chase & Co. https://www.jpmorganchase.com/corporate/news/stories/how-long-to-advance-women.htm

118 "Making the Invisible Visible." Deloitte Insights. https://www2.deloitte.com/insights/us/en/focus/technologyand-the-future-of-work/organizational-network-analysis-network-of-teams.html

119 "Lunch Roulette FAQs." Lunch Roulette. https://lunchroulette.us/faq.html

120 Downie, Alan. "Bro, Ditch the Ping Pong Tables." Medium. January 20, 2017. https://medium.com/startupgrind/bro-ditch-the-table-tennis-5ff05cde65b8

121 "The Wage Gap for Women of Color Widened in 2017." National Women's Law Center. https://nwlc.org/blog/the-wage-gap-for-women-of-color-widened-in-2017/

122 "Women on Corporate Boards." Catalyst. December 21, 2018. https:// www.catalyst.org/knowledge/womencorporate-boards#footnote33_wkynwps

123 "Women on Corporate Boards." Catalyst. December 21, 2018. https:// www.catalyst.org/knowledge/womencorporate-boards#footnote33_wkynwps

124 "These Countries Have the Most Women in Parliament." World Economic Forum. February 12, 2019. https://www.weforum.org/agenda/2019/02/ chart-of-the-day-these-countries-have-the-most-women-inparliament/

125 "Melinda Gates is Proud Women are Becoming More Empowered—But It's Not Happening Fast Enough." Town & Country. May 8, 2019. https:// www.townandcountrymag.com/society/money-and-power/a27324587/ melindagates-moment-of-lift-cover-interview-john-legend/

126 "The Simple Truth About the Gender Pay Gap." American Association of University Women (AAUW). Fall 2018. https://www.aauw.org/aauw_check/ pdf_download/show_pdf.php?file=simple-truth-one-pager

127 "10 Facts About American Women in the Workforce." The Brookings Institution. https://www.brookings.edu/blog/brookings-now/2017/12/05/10-facts-about-american-women-in-the-workforce/

128 "The Simple Truth About the Gender Pay Gap." American Association of University Women (AAUW). Fall 2018. https://www.aauw.org/aauw_check/ pdf_download/show_pdf.php?file=simple-truth-one-pager

129 "The Economic Impact of Equal Pay by State." Institute for Women's Policy Research. https://statusofwomendata.org/featured/the-economic-impact-of-equal-pay-by-state/

130 "The Simple Truth About the Gender Pay Gap." American Association of University Women (AAUW). Fall 2018. https://www.aauw.org/aauw_check/ pdf_download/show_pdf.php?file=simple-truth-one-pager

131 "CEO Insights: Why Closing the Gender Pay Gap Could Save Social Security." Bloomberg Live. December 11, 2018. https://www.bloomberglive.com/ blog/ceo-insights-closing-gender-pay-gap-save-social-security/

132 "Research: Gender Pay Gaps Shrink When Companies Are Required to Disclose Them." Harvard Business Review. January 23, 2019. https://hbr.org/2019/01/ research-gender-pay-gaps-shrink-when-companies-arerequired-to-disclose-them

133 "2019 Salesforce Equal Pay Update." Salesforce. https://www.salesforce.com/ blog/2019/04/equal-pay-update2019.html

134 "A Response to Why Companies' Attempts to Close the Gender Pay Gap Often Fail." Medium. January 25, 2019. https://medium.com/@colacurcio.maria/a-corporate-response-to-why-companies-attempts-to-close-the-genderpay-gap-often-fail-b02eaf60a6dc

135 "Countries Implement New Gender Pay Gap Measures." International Labor and Employment Law. November 27, 2018. https://www.internationallaborlaw. com/2018/11/27/countries-implement-new-gender-pay-gapmeasures/

136 "Pay Equity and Discrimination." Institute for Women's Policy Research. https://iwpr.org/issue/employmenteducation-economic-change/pay-equity-discrimination/

137 "Gender Pay Reporting May Start in Weeks Across Corporate America." Bloomberg. March 6, 2019. https://www.bloomberg.com/news/articles/2019-03-06/u-s-companies-told-to-report-gender-racial-pay-data-toeeoc

138 "Starbucks Announces 100% Gender, Racial Pay Equity for U.S. Partners, Sets Global Commitment." Starbucks Press Release. March 21, 2018. https://stories.starbucks.com/stories/2018/starbucks-pay-equity-for-partners/

139 "Accenture Ranks No. 1 on Thomson Reuters Index of World's Most Diverse and Inclusive Companies." Accenture Press Release. September 6, 2018. https://newsroom.accenture.com/news/accenture-ranks-no-1-onthomson-reuters-index-of-worlds-most-diverse-and-inclusive-companies.htm

140 "About Pipeline." Pipeline. https://www.pipelineequity.com/company/

141 "How it Works." Pipeline. https://www.pipelineequity.com/how-it-works/

142 "Katica's Voice." Pipeline. https://www.pipelineequity.com/company/

143 "Angela Duckworth Q&A." Angela Duckworth. https://angeladuckworth.com/qa/

144 "Get the GA Tally App." GenderAvenger. https://www.GenderAvenger.com/tally

145 "Stamps of Approval." GenderAvenger. https://www.GenderAvenger.com/stamp-of-approval

146 "GenderAvenger Letter to the Consumer Technology Association." December 18, 2018. https://static1.squarespace.com/static/52d48817e4b02a4ced94d551/t/5c19be1a0ebbe8ea639e8477/1545190939686/CES+letter+12-18.pdf

147 "About Parity." Parity. https://parity.org/about-us/

148 "Ruth Bader Ginsburg Tells Young Women: 'Fight for the Things You Care About.'" Radcliffe Institute for Advanced Study, Harvard University. https://www.radcliffe.harvard.edu/news/in-news/ruth-bader-ginsburg-tellsyoung-women-fight-things-you-care-about

149 Kaufman Michael. The Time Has Come: Why Men Must Join the Gender Equality Revolution. Page 25.

150 Kaufman Michael. The Time Has Come: Why Men Must Join the Gender Equality Revolution. Page 6.

INDEX

Printed in the United States
By Bookmasters